HEALING EVERY DAY

From Daily Routines Into Self-Healing Rituals
Imaginations and Exercises

DR. ALEXANDRA KLEEBERG

BALBOA.
PRESS

A DIVISION OF HAY HOUSE

Scripture taken from the King James Version of the Bible.

Balboa Press books may be ordered through booksellers or by contacting:

Balboa Press
A Division of Hay House
1663 Liberty Drive
Bloomington, IN 47403
www.balboapress.com
1 (877) 407-4847

Because of the dynamic nature of the Internet, any web addresses or links contained in this book may have changed since publication and may no longer be valid. The views expressed in this work are solely those of the author and do not necessarily reflect the views of the publisher, and the publisher hereby disclaims any responsibility for them.

The author of this book does not dispense medical advice or prescribe the use of any technique as a form of treatment for physical, emotional, or medical problems without the advice of a physician, either directly or indirectly. The intent of the author is only to offer information of a general nature to help you in your quest for emotional and spiritual well-being. In the event you use any of the information in this book for yourself, which is your constitutional right, the author and the publisher assume no responsibility for your actions.

Stock Imagery: Fotolia, Shutterstock, Deposit Photos
Flickr: Alice Popcorn, jinterwas

Print information available on the last page.

ISBN: 978-1-5043-9443-7 (sc)
ISBN: 978-1-5043-9444-4 (hc)
ISBN: 978-1-5043-9442-0 (e)

Library of Congress Control Number: 2018900270

Balboa Press rev. date: 07/02/2018

*May the blessing of the rising sun
that lightens the morning
watch over your steps this day.
May the blessing of the setting sun
that warms the evening
guide your sleep and your dreams.*[1]

This book is intended for people who actively want to take charge of their health. It serves to liberate the body and soul from tensions and fears, and to concentrate the awareness on a fulfilled present and future. The various techniques, exercises, and attitudes will inspire you to access your very own power, creativity, and inner wisdom. Trust in this power so that your own healing potential can be found, strengthened, and developed.

The exercises can be practiced either alone or combined with other techniques. In the case of a medical diagnosis, they offer support alongside other treatments. A balanced body and soul full of joy are equipped with increased possibilities for convalescence.

In addition, please read, view, and hear some further information on my homepage http://evisionpublishing.com. There you will find audios and videos, a look inside my other books, as well as workshop dates.

I have practiced all of the following exercises in regular group meetings and in many workshops. I have received steady feedback about how and when they have the best effect. The imaginations, which are summarized here, are the essence of helpful practices for self-healing in everyday life.

In order for the techniques to develop their effectiveness, you must deepen the access to your inner world and then practice, practice, practice. The good news is most of the exercises in this book won't take a lot of additional time. You can integrate them into your daily routines so they become healing rituals. With an enthused will in the creative field of awareness, with an open heart in the space of authentic sensation, and with a deep trust in the ancient wisdom of the body, self-healing can be successful.

THANK YOU

Thanks to all the creative powers of this world and to the large number of people who provided me access to it. They are scattered across the continents. From them I have learned to trust my own sensation, authenticity, and creativity.

Thanks in particular to the participants of my groups. They have inspired me to deepen my experiences, to expand my knowledge, and to always find the way back to my heart. They have helped me to marvel at the wonders that are possible when we engage in our own authenticity and creative freedom. Then our inner wisdom starts to bubble spontaneously and deepens and widens our daily lives

Thanks to all the loved ones around me who keep me, take care of me, and nurse me. Thanks also to those who challenge, test, and affect me.

Thanks to all who participated in the writing of this book, especially Marion Wolters for the translation, Keidi Keating for extra polishing, and Dietrich Busacker for his inspirations and warm support. Thank you Balboa Press for editing.

Now is always the most wonderful blink of an eye.

CONTENTS

The Times, they are A-Changing

*"Fantasy is the golden shine which lies over the existence
and which rises over the greyness of everyday life."*
—*Wladimir Lindenberg*

Would you like to heal without investing too much time? Would you like to recover during your daily routine? Would you like to transform during your nights? Would you like to change, deepen, expand, and center your life? Would you like to live in rhythm with yourself and with all there is?

The earth and the stars have always set our rhythm. We call the period the earth requires for turning around itself "day" and "night," or *nychthemeron*. For all the other smaller divisions, the cosmos does not have any standards for us. So it seems that the Sumerians have already dissected time in hours some five thousand years ago. It was probably somewhere in the middle of the fourteenth century that the hour became an official quantity. The seconds counter was added only with the rise of industrialization in the eighteenth century. Therefore, today a day counts 24 hours or 1,440 minutes or 86,400 seconds.

What an abundance of time! What do you do with it? Do you let it slip away? Do you fill it up? Do you shape it? Do you take your time so it is really yours?

The phenomenon of time remains one of the best-kept secrets of the world. The ancient Greeks even gave time divine faces; it was often something holy, so it was something healing. "Time heals all wounds" is another vernacular expression we all know. Time, as such, can nearly be denominated as an archetype—an unconscious pattern of ideas that structures us from inside and straightens our lives in a way. The nature of this archetype is unconscious and can only be experienced in its effect and in its symbolic meaning.

This archetype is subject to the changing times. Today we are living in a very special space-time. In past centuries, not only the zeitgeist changed but also our understanding of time, our time structure, and its contents changed. Life is not the same as it was centuries ago. Time appears quicker and shorter, but it is perhaps more efficient and goal-oriented too. We think that we have less time at our disposal, although we have much more free time during the day and in the overall picture of our lives.

All these changes also have an influence on our everyday lives and often drive us to live hastily. This modified world creates and nourishes many chronic diseases. They are symptoms—cries for help of today's time.

The phenomenon of time has shaped time in the way we regard it right now. Billions of years ago, space-time exploded into life. Very many years later we - the human race - gave them divine faces. We drove on their carriages through the rhythms of day and night. In the course of time, the gods of time were dethroned and murdered; time itself became their butcher. While digitalization increased, time was cut up—and then it went on to cut up us. We call this condition "burnout"—the flame of time almost expired.

In modern times, we have fallen out of the rhythms of time and life. We are living in a time where rituals have started to break up; it is a time of decomposition of both individual and social healing and nourishing time structures. Not only do we have shift work, with its dissolution of rhythms, but we also have inventions that are apparently neutral to time, such as the light bulb, the airplane, medicine, and so on. All of these deeply influence how we experience time. If you search for more examples, you will definitely find them. Just look around.

When the times are changing, it's time to change ourselves, as well.

Time as an archetype has two sides: one, where it runs out and decomposes, and two, where it deepens and completes us. In business life, "time is money." Simultaneously, procedures come into our collective consciousness that can stop time, as inspired awareness, and open the gates to now or the flow into creativity. Thus, we can be liberated from the entanglements of time until only the essence of time remains—the moment that is open, fulfilled, and creative here and now.

Our body, with its trillions of pieces of wisdom, is still swinging in the rhythms of the world, which have surrounded it naturally, and time still accompanies it despite all modernity. The recurring rhythms of day and night have caused us, as living creatures, to develop a multitude of inner clocks; these inner clocks have to be synchronized repeatedly in today's modern world. Recovery will be affected in harmony with these rhythms.

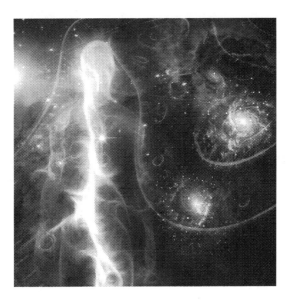

Therefore, in this book we connect with the rhythms of day and night and draw from their symbolic depth. Every day and every night, we dispose of profound symbolic and healing insight. Every dawn shines through our confidence, and every sunset floods our farewell. Every night shelters us, and every day enlightens us. In the light of the sun and in the sparkling of the stars, the cells of our bodies are stimulated to live in the rhythm. With every sunray, we internalize warmth and light; with every starry sky, we absorb the dark width of apparent endlessness. We swing in resonance with it.

In the following explanations and exercises, we will awaken these old rhythms anew. As the suggested practices are often exercises of imagination, you can even do them if you are not in the forest or in the sunshine. You can imagine being in an airplane between two time zones, in a high-rise building, or even in a cellar.

Inside you will find access. Your inner wisdom knows the sunrise, the zenith, the setting sun, and the night. Elicit these pictures, and nourish them, and then they will nourish you. Yes, they will satiate and fulfill you.

We are linking the natural rhythms with various trainings that are mostly exercises of imagination. In our realm of fantasy, we are creators of our lives where we can reign and rule and develop our creativity to the fullest extent. So we can make the source of time divine again and bind ourselves to it in order to find ourselves a home in the time. "Our true home is the current moment," expressed Thich Nhat Hanh, a well-known Buddhist monk.

Just as if the whole evolution of this universe seems to be revealed in this very moment, imagine its subtle information in a drop of water, in every molecule, and in every atom swinging across the entire cosmos.

In this drop, which you might possibly drink in a moment, you can notice that it mirrors its surroundings. It can also mirror time; you might see the deep kiss of two atoms, the fantastic creation of the young earth, or the evolution of living creatures, all of which have been developed out of the water. They have taken the ocean water with them just inside. You can sense it dancing in your cells and all around. You can even experience yourself through this drop—a fluid pearl in the choppy ocean we call life, separate and deeply connected with all there is.

In every moment, you can look into the depth of this world and shape it. For this purpose, you leave your everyday consciousness, which likes to get lost in the dimensions of time, and you look inside, recognize, and transform.

Actually, it is quite easy. It is simply about changing your attitude during your daily routine—your thoughts, sensations, feelings, inner pictures, and most of all, posture. Push away the veil of dull routines, make your way out, and begin an enthusiastic life, just like in the following exercise.

In this exercise, we will develop healing imaginations. In order for you to realize them directly, I have *italicized* them. It is better that you close your eyes, although your eyes will need to be open so that you can continue reading. So please understand the text first, and then shut your eyes and dive into your inner world of pictures. Enjoy it! Shape it! You are the creator of your very own life!

In the case above, you might imagine it this way:

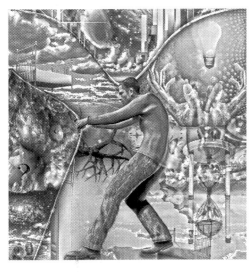

Please close your dear eyes. See the veil, shadow, and fog that surround you and spin a cocoon of dullness around you. Experience apathy, loneliness, and fear.

Then start to shape. Lift the veil of your existence, and as you exhale, blow away the fog that wraps around your soul. Break the chains that hold you back, or break down the walls.

Breathe out! Look! The sun rises, lightens your darkness, and enlightens your mind. Let it become light in your heart. Go out and play! Move yourself and feel free forever.

Such a metamorphosis or transformation does not happen via your intellect but via your inspiration and enthusiasm. The brain is inspired by enthusiasm to create new neuronal networks and, along with this, new experiences.

If you do not feel enthusiastic right now, then remember or create enthusiasm. We all have lived through feelings of enthusiasm, fascination, and curious anticipation. Go back in your childhood, where you will probably find some of them. Just remember the warm love of your mother or the tender shelter of your father. Remember Christmas, a tasty ice cream cone, or your first love. If you cannot find any nourishing pictures in your real life, then just imagine them as if they were real. Imagine you are a child who is cared for. Imagine being the friend of Buddha. Imagine experiencing the deep joy of the morning birds. Or just take Julia Roberts's smile, and put it on your face. Connect yourself with healing pictures to anchor the new experiences. Bring these pictures in your body. Embody enthusiasm.

Start to jump, cheer, and beam!

As soon as your body gets moving, thoughts and sensations start to form a river of the enthused life, which the psychology calls "flow." It is not important for your body, whether you believe in your own enthusiasm right now or you doubt it. As long as your body is imitating a jumping movement, and the corners of your mouth move up toward your ears, your body is releasing "happy hormones," which strengthen and deepen your anticipation.

This will have a deep effect on your inner attitude toward yourself, the people you meet, and even the things around you.

You do not need to sip your coffee hastily any longer.

You may enjoy it now.

Moreover, you can feel better in your body and lead it into a new posture for finally shaping your own creativity into the daily routine. Therefore, you do not need to solve problems, but to abandon them.

You may now bind the neuronal networks (which have tied your brain with the everyday routine) with awakening, joy, and creativity. In addition, an individual melody is flooding through your activities in a healing way. I have composed a lot of music in these pages as an example, as much as is possible within the frame of a book. Many of the chapter titles are song titles, so you can sort of dance through this book. Music—particularly your favorite music—connects your brain to the special phases of life. With music, the weaving of a new network is often easier.

From the possibly countless visual memories your brain produces every day, these healing pictures will guide you into hidden worlds inside yourself. Moreover, I will tell you stories again and again and plunge you into the mythology of ancient cultures. Please be inspired by the pictures. Stories are like mirrors—they provide possibilities for a solution, offer protection, can easily be remembered, inspire fantasy, and create closeness to our culture.

Please also find some listening exercises for further inspiration on amazon.

Even when the clock is running, your deep look inside will change your daily experience of time. If you take your time it might even see that time will grow and space will widen.

Stress narrows not only time but space. You may feel that physically when you hardly manage to inhale enough air to breathe.

When time is becoming scarcer, it is helpful to give space to time, which means to lend sense and possibilities to it. We will fill this space with ancient and modern sounds, poems, and myths, as well as the beauty of day and night. We will stabilize this by doing daily exercises that are connected to the rhythms of the time. In the womb of these reliabilities you can develop. I hope that you find that many daily tasks become easier and easier. Your days will become more fulfilled, and happiness will find its way into your reality more often so that your life starts to become successful, healing, whole, and holy.

I will introduce a first song, "Father of Day, Father of Night." In 1970, Bob Dylan wrote it as an anthem about his Jewish heritage, but it only became famous a few years later, when Manfred Mann's Earth Band performed it. Because you might not agree with a Jewish or Christian god, I will give you my own neutral version:

Wisdom of night, wisdom of day
Wisdom, who taketh the darkness away

...

Wisdom of time, wisdom of dreams,
Wisdom, who turneth the rivers and streams

...

Wisdom of minutes, wisdom of days
Wisdom we most solemnly praise.

TAKE YOUR TIME

Take care on this day, as it is your life.[2]

Flickr: Alice Popcorn - Guardian of time

Welcome to this wonderland, the land of possibilities in which wonders happen every day and the great secret of life reveals itself. Do you sense the sunrise, whose rays are caressing you carefully? Do you enlighten your midday with clarity, power, and awareness? Do you worship the width of the starry heavens, which opens your soul?

Fulfill your wonderful body with the magic of the day and the magic of the night until it shines, beams, and twinkles like a diamond that breaks the rhythm of time in the colors of the rainbow. Experience how it reveals its knowledge about healing, luck, wholeness, closeness, harmony, and balance, until you know, feel, and intuit the power of time—transformed, fulfilled, creative and always whole. Awake for this very moment!

In this way you can dream about your day and enlighten your night. What are you doing right now? Surely you are reading this book! Maybe you want to put it down right now, thinking that you have to do something better. You don't have the time!

However, maybe you are also fascinated by a particular curiosity, and this is what keeps you reading. I wish you the enthusiasm for the whole width, depth, and fullness of this moment, and I hope that you have the feeling of a home in time that you can trust. I imagine you as happy, healthy, and open for all the wonders of the world and the magic of time.

Right now? In this moment? Yes, now! Pause for a moment. Look around. Where are you? In a bookshop? At home on the sofa? Or in the middle of a colorful meadow? Have a look at the sun. Do you sense the rays tickling your skin? Or do you breathe in the smell of boiling tea? Do you drink the colorful world of pictures of the four seasons? Do you internalize your life? Do you want to externalize your existence?

Maybe you know the following story: A wise man was asked curiously, "You are very busy, but you're always concentrated. What is your secret?" He answered directly and clear. "If I stand, I stand. If I go, I go. If I sit, I sit. If I eat, I eat. If I speak, I speak." He was interrupted hastily. "We do the same thing. Why are you lucky with all that and we are not?" The wise man remarked, "Maybe this is the reason. If you stand, you are already walking. When you walk, you are already running. When you run, you are already at the goal."

What about you? Are you already planning your next duty while you are reading these words? Are you brooding over your past, or are you looking anxiously into your future? Are you here in this moment or somewhere else or even nowhere?

You are breathing—that's for sure. Your heart is beating. Your wonderful body is metabolizing within one hundred thousand biochemical processes a second. And while you are reading this, every thought, sensation, and attitude is having an impact on the biochemistry of your blood, on the neuronal network in your brain, on your mood, on your posture, on your environment, and even on the unfathomable depths of this world. What is happening in your spirit is echoing throughout the whole universe. That is what the Tibetans already knew.

Please shut your eyes. Allow pictures, colors, and sensations to arise in your thoughts. Visualize how they flood your whole body, emerge from it, and waft around the earth until they apparently (but only apparently) get lost in space.

Every one of your sensations changes and shapes your life, those of your loved ones, and last but not least the life of mankind.

"What a responsibility!" you might moan. Yes, what a great responsibility, but also, what a chance!

Stop for a moment. Please close your eyes.
Breathe out. Liberate yourself from all that is old, unnecessary, painful, agonizing, and dark. Breathe out. What do you experience in this very moment? What is now? How does this moment smell and taste? How does it

feel? How does it look? How does it sound? On what do you concentrate your attention? What meaning do you give these sensations?

Stop for a moment. Who are you? Whom or what are you observing in this period of time? When you can watch this moment then you are more than this blink of an eye. Who are you?

Stop for a moment. Where do you want to go? What kind of sensations would you like to create? How do you want to create your presence and determine the course for your future?

Stop for a moment. Breathe out the fears of the past and the worries of the future. Breathe in freedom. Experience yourself in the center of these blissful visions. Relax in the very midst of them.

Luck is like a butterfly. If you hunt it, you will not be able to catch it. But if you keep quiet for a moment, it will alight on you.[3]

"Oh, now I know what you're getting at," I can hear you say. "You want to exercise mindfulness with me, true?"

The mindfulness exercises that are known today are often attributed to Buddhism. We can find them in most ancient spiritual traditions. These exercises promote awareness for the body, the sensations, the spirit, and the objects of the spirit.

The term "mindfulness" became well-known by Jon Kabat-Zinn. Jon Kabat-Zinn, a molecular biologist, is the son of an immunologist. Through his own experiences and scientific experiments, he investigated the positive impact of mindfulness on our immune system and our mental state. In the meantime, we can assume that mindfulness can cause an improved regulation of emotions by inhibiting the center of fear in the brain. Therefore, mindfulness exercises are an integral part of many ambulant and stationary treatments, retreats, and coaching practices.

According to Jon Kabat-Zinn, a special kind of consciousness is impartial and related to the current moment. In contrast to concentration, which narrows the sensation for a particular task, consciousness widens for a view of the whole, a wide-angle panorama attitude, open like the firmament.[4] Mindfulness opens the energy of curiosity, open-mindedness, and the joy to make discoveries.

Please shut your dear eyes. Visualize the situations in your life when you sunk into yourself and melted with the environment at the same time, when your heart and your spirit were opening wide and fulfilled. How were your posture, your view, your thoughts, and your sensation of the world? Please write down these results, and remember them forever. Let them be the criterion for coming experiences.

There are thousands of books about mindfulness. Now you are looking a bit bored. You are probably saying, "I have some of them at home, and to be honest, I haven't read them all ..." You consider putting this book aside or, in the best case, adding it to your to-do list. "Sometime, when I'm a pensioner, I'll have the time to get my teeth into it. Maybe even on my next vacation. But to be honest, I prefer a good crime story. I have to divert from everyday stress. It's true that I'm interested in it, and I really believe it will help me. But now, in this moment in my life, I don't have time. I should have done so many other things today. And now I have dreamed my life away by reading your book. Time is running out!" you shout, feeling stressed out, and you point a finger at your watch impatiently.

Okay, I will get to the point now. Sure, you are right. Time is money, and the sack will get fuller if we learn to expand and deepen time. Then the treasures of time will sparkle at us. You should relax every time you do not have time for it, shouldn't you?

So please give me a chance, and give me the time to tell you another story. It goes like this: Two monks meet during their break in the monastery garden. One of them is sitting on a bank in praying contemplation and smoking. The other one is indignant about it. "But, brother, we are not allowed to smoke while praying." "No problem," he responds, relaxed. "I have the explicit permission of the master." Some weeks later, the two meet again. The young monk moans, "What did you tell me? I have asked our master whether I may smoke while praying, and he has forbidden it strictly." The monk looks at him, smiling. "Yes, however, I have asked him whether I can pray while smoking."

What a subtle but profound difference, don't you think? If we are not allowed to smoke while praying, but we are allowed to pray will smoking, what does this mean for us?

We do not have to retire in a hermitage for praying and healing. We can use everything in our everyday life for praying—every handwashing, every ice cream eating, every coffee brewing, and every rocking of a song. We may pray during all of these activities. We may wrap all actions of our everyday life into a holy and healing melody, which connects every step and every breath with the source of creation. And if you do not like to pray, I invite you to my everyday rituals with healing pictures. You might call them spiritual, but you might also just call them helpful.

You can shape an exercise for your self-healing out of almost any daily activity. Just connect your awareness through an umbilical cord to the fantastic depths of this creative universe. Carl Gustav Jung calls this the symbolic life.

"We all urgently require the symbolic life. Only the symbolic life can express the daily requirements of the soul. And as people do not possess anything like that, they can never get off their treadmill, out of this terrible, trivial life that wears them down. Life is too rational. There is no symbolic existence in which I am someone different, where I can play a role as one of the actors in the divine drama of life. There is an inner peace when people feel that they are living this symbolic life, that they are actors in the divine drama. This is the only thing that lends a sense to human life; everything else is trivial, and you can leave it aside."[5]

Hermann Hesse, who incidentally is a pupil of Carl Gustav Jung, expresses in his fairy tale *Iris*, "Every phenomenon on earth is an allegory and every allegory is an open gate through which the soul, when it is prepared, can go into the interior of the world where you and I, day and night are one. However, only a few go through this gate and give away the beautiful appearances for a suspected reality inside."

Look around. You can see objects; you can sense colors and smells; and you can recognize movements and track events. Around you is the world of objects, which is familiar to you and me. In the Eastern religions this world outside is described as *Maya*. *Maya* is Sanskrit and means "illusion" or "magic." *Maya* is also the goddess of blindness, as well as the goddess of creative energy. As a goddess, *Maya* is the mother of the world, the creator of the universe, the universe itself, and the goddess of illusion. She acts as the world's weaver who has created herself and everything that is manifest. Therefore, the symbols of *Maya* are the seven colors of the rainbow, the veil, and the cobweb.

In many traditions *Maya* is connected to the highest power, as inseparable as heat and fire, moisture and water, or life and healing. *Maya* is the veil and the gate at the same time. Like the door, *Maya* is also the transition. As our senses are the swing doors for the interior and the exterior, *Maya* is connected to not only the illusions of the world but also its original productive creativity.

What is real? The world of matter, the book you are reading, the chair on which you are sitting, and the cake you are eating? The world of spirit, the vision you develop, the realizations that you collect, and the sensations you are directing? After thousands of years full of discussions about the priority of spirit or matter, quantum physics has decided unambiguously on the primacy of the spirit. Beyond or within the world of matter we will find molecules, then atoms, and last but not least oscillation.

In my book, *Das Buch der Selbstheilung, The Book of Self-Healing*, I called this deep layer of existence the ocean of creation, which in physics is often referred to as the quantum field or vacuum field. There we are formed in its waves, in its depths and widths, and we are dissolving into our origin: pure energy.

Today's scientific worldview is that the human spirit forms and informs the deep oscillations of the world. In our daily lives we still assume and experience the separation of spirit and matter. There we feel isolated and lonely.

Carl Gustav Jung ascribes this sensed isolation to the dehumanization of the world via a one-sided sensible understanding. So we human beings have lost our unconscious identity with the appearance of nature, which has lost its symbolic contents bit by bit over the centuries.

> "The thunder is no longer the voice of a thundering god and the flash of lightning no longer his punishing missile. A ghost is not living any longer in the river, no tree is the life principle of a man, no snail is the embodiment of wisdom, no mountain cave is the flat of a great demon. No voices in the stones, plants, and animals speak to the people and talk to them believing that they understand them. The contact to nature got lost and with it the strong

emotional energy this symbolic connection might have effected."[6]

Today we know that loneliness only happens in our heads. The German mystic Meister Eckhart already got to the heart of it: "God is always in us, but we are only seldom at home."

On a deeper level however we are always connected to everything. In the ocean of creation, we are white crests in weaving waves.

Please close your dear eyes. Breathe out your daily routine. Breathe in relaxation. Watch the rhythm of your breath, the lifting and lowering of your trunk. With the apparent routine of these waves, let yourself bear into the widths of the ocean waves. Weave in the middle of the ocean. Sense widths and freedom. Then sink down to the hidden streams of your existence. There you can dissolve as a drop in the ocean. Vanish into all waters. Be the ocean.

A symbol connects the white crests of the waves and the depths of creation. In Greek, *symbol* means "to coincide, to assemble," and it probably refers to this umbilical cord between the worlds. In contrast to that in the *diabolo* (the devil), things fall apart. The symbol connects us to the fullness that we are and that is available to us. Its center is the archetype, a source of energy.

Please shut your dear eyes. Attract your caring attention inside, to your heart. Breathe in and breathe out through your heart. Sense your physical heart and how it pumps and pounds. Then visualize the golden umbilical cord and the symbolic lying behind it. Feel it connected to your innermost love. Breathe in love, and exhale love.

Would you like to go on a discovery mission and exercise at the same time to connect the worlds and to recharge the routine with beauty and fullness? Come with me and dive into the symbolic life as you discover the magic of the world behind the world. This way the routine becomes a shaping room in which healing can be experienced.

You can start with the following exercise, and then you can shift into the so-called real world. You can shape an exercise for your self-healing in almost all your daily life activities.

Get up! Do not only get up in a conscious way, but get up in your dignity. Enter the realm in which you are the creator of your life. Look with your inner eye above. Within a golden ray your crown is lit up and shiny. If you like, let your wings grow, expansive and wide, ready to take off. Widen your thorax. Open your heart for the present moment and the depth of time. Breathe out old things, and breathe in the living present. Take the sun of your life into your own hands.

How often in a day do you get up (get up from your bed, get up from the toilet, get up from dressing, get up from the dining table, get out of the car, get up from the chair, get up in your office, or get up from the recliner)? If you add it up, you will see that it is numerous times.

You can celebrate every "getting up" as a symbolic act of exercising your dignity, joy, curiosity, eroticism, courage, or calmness. Choose for yourself. "How do I come into my dignity?" you might ask. It's quite easy. Imagine that you are getting up like a king, queen, saint, or master. Get into a graceful posture. You are upright, noble, and self-assured. Sense the dignity of your body and your whole existence. Balance the crown on your head, and see your wings swinging in the wind of freedom.

I wrote the main part of this book in my five-square-yard mini office on the fourth floor. I often forgot something downstairs—a pen, a cup of tea, or a book, or I forgot to answer a question one of my children asked me. This kept me busy, and I sometimes moaned about my absentmindedness. "Those who can't use their head must use their back," my parents used to say to me. At that time, I apologized or justified or simply hunched my shoulders.

Sometimes when the pressure to justify dissolved in creative inspiration, I simply reworded the sentence a little: "Those who can't use their empty head need to move instead." And with this I have changed my posture for getting up and climbing stairs. I exercised my flexibility and agility. Without this forgetfulness, I would not have moved from my desk at all!

I hope you understand what I mean. Get up!

If you like, sing and dance with Pink:

> *Where there is desire*
> *There is gonna be a flame*
> *You've gotta get up and try try try*
> *Gotta get up and try try try.*[7]

Sure, you are allowed to sit down. You have as many opportunities to exercise sitting down as you do getting up. Isn't it fantastic? You can take a seat in calmness, confidence, wisdom, and dedication. You decide for yourself!

What happens between getting up and sitting down? Probably exhaling! Sense the moment of change and the new direction. Decide for yourself!

You can creatively shape an activity. You can transform it into an exercise of beauty, learning, and magic. Transformation means remodeling. However, we achieve another level. We change the daily routine into a ritual of healing where we can recover. And we do not require any extra time. It is just the opposite; we dock our deep meaning with the automatism we have already learned. Then the new behavior can be saved. We expand time while we deepen it. We float into a flow where we rejuvenate.

So now I have given you a little taste of the coming exercises. They are well linked to your daily routine, as well as to your swinging rhythms of day and night. They are connected to the depths of your heart and the widths of this world. May they bless your time on earth.

If you would like to start with the exercises now, please skip the next pages and continue with the chapter "Instructions for Everyday Practice".

If you want to get to know more about the interweaving of mankind in the circles of the cosmos, then take your time and read more. Snuggle up in every moment so that it can rock you. Look inside so that your innermost part can hold you!

TIME AFTER TIME

*"All your hours are wings that beat
through space - from self to self."*
—*Khalil Gibran*

"Why now? I don't have any time for this excursion," you might say. I have asked myself the same question.

While I am writing about time, it's flying. My fingers are striking the keyboard of matter, while my mind is rushing ahead in the vision of an idea. In this split second, time squeaks by. And then this issue has cost me a lot of arduous time on another level.

My computer has swallowed complete paragraphs of written text and has not given them back. Where have they gone? Where is the time? Where does the expression of time in the form of words remain? They were neither in the recycling bin, nor in the drafts, nor recorded somewhere else. I had to reword some sentences and create some paragraphs again and again on the basis of what I still remembered, just like the scene in the film *Groundhog Day*. And then, *whoosh*, they disappeared again. For some reason the computer could not save them.

Fortunately, this happened only while writing this chapter. Carl Gustav Jung would call this phenomenon "meaningful synchronicity." However, angry at the loss of the pages, and the computer's and my own incompetence, I could not see any sense in this expression of synchronicity for the time being.

When I decided to rewrite everything, I suddenly felt the possible meaning behind this incident. The strain was probably worth this entire story. You probably know how the minutes pass and you do not save your material. On the one hand, time flew by. I always reached over to grab it, but I caught nothing—only emptiness.

The room is visible. You can sense it and maybe even hear it, but can you see, hear, smell, and taste the time? Probably not, as it is not part of our senses. However, it can be experienced through our sensual experiences. Is it only a construct? Does it even exist? What we are experiencing is a series of present moments.

Past and future exist only in our memories, visions, books, or essays. And even they are only present in the presence, too.

Please shut your dear eyes now. Focus your loving attention on your heart, and ask the wisdom of your heart this question: What is time? Listen to the answer.

Why were these five pages I wrote about time simply nowhere to be found? Maybe the loss of materialized time in the form of text will inspire me to appreciate more the preciousness of time, to deal with it in a more careful way, and to fulfill it more mindfully. Maybe the disappearance of time will help me to let it go, not to adhere to it, as Buddhism teaches.

To be honest, until now I did not think about the phenomenon of time very much. I have simply taken my time, as it seemed to me, and lived as you may too. The term "time" (and probably time itself) is exceedingly multilayered and complex. Even at the end of these explanations, we appear out of the jungle of different temporalities, look around, and where do we touch down? Directly in the presence!

Please close your dear eyes. Imagine time in an hourglass, and watch how it goes grain by grain. Recall your life, and observe how every second of your life passes by ... until now. Experience how even the moment just before has now gone. Experience the unstoppable aspect of time. In doing so, how does your body feel? Look again at your hourglass. You have transformed time into experienced life. It is yours! While time is passing, the mountain of life is growing taller. Abundance grows.

TIME FOR YOURSELF

"The sum of our life are the hours in which we loved."
—Erich Kästner

Just as we require time to make us unhappy and ill, we also require time to heal. Depending on the symptoms and condition, we can take extra time for ourselves in addition to the rituals of our everyday routine. Later, when we have internalized everything and made it automatic, we will simply flow into the applicable exercises during our everyday life—at the bus stop, in the traffic jam, and in the supermarket queue. But first we must exercise with cheering discipline and an enthusiastic will. Enthusiasm is the fertilizer for the brain, research confirms. With enthusiasm the nerve cells come together and shape a creative texture of our personality.

So please take time for introspection, sensing, and developing. It's a time to listen to yourself, to take yourself seriously, to recognize your own voice, and to enter into a dialogue with it.

Please shut your dear eyes. Take time for your interior, truthfulness, creativity, and fullness, which is waiting to awaken in your center.

Do you know the book *Momo*? Michael Ende wrote this fairytale-like novel toward the end of 1973. Maybe you have seen the film that was made in 1986 by Johannes Schaaf with the wonderful music of Angelo Branduardi. Let us sit down on the banks of the ocean of creation and listen to the story of the time thieves, about the child who brings back the stolen time to the human beings.

Momo, a little girl, nearly a childlike tramp, appears all of a sudden in an Italian town, neglected but very bright. Her absolute specialty is "having time, taking time, and listening." She wins the hearts of the people, and she even hears what their hearts say. The town's inhabitants enjoy time with Momo. They pour out their hearts to her, and in this touching entrustment they are mirrored by how independent, fascinating and strong they are and how extensive their lives are.

One day, cigar-smoking grey gentlemen in cobweb-colored dresses with lead briefcases appear, in whose presence the people are shivering. The grey men are very good at "time"-sucking. They persuade people that they are only allowed to do profitable things in order to save as much time as possible. The time saved will then be put into an account at the time-saving bank. The men from the time-saving bank live off the stolen time of the people. They suck dry the people's lifetime. For example, the haircutter who overslept more than 100 0000 hours in his life, who ate for about 40 000 hours, who helped his old mother for more than 10 000 hours and wasted about the same amount of time for the wooing of a seemingly unreachable woman. What a waste of time! After this frightening talk, the haircutter now cuts his customers' hair in twenty minutes rather than thirty minutes. He doesn't care for his mother any more and only little for this adorable woman.

So the people now declare their time to the time-saving bank, and Momo is growing lonelier as people do not have the time any longer to tell her their stories. Despite that, they are getting richer, more stressed, and terribly unapproachable.

One of the grey gentlemen speaks to Momo. "You must always have more and more. Then you will never be bored," he argues. But when Momo asks him whether somebody is fond of him, he convulses with agony and struggles, explaining that he and his equals could not exist without the human beings' saved time credit.

In need, Momo turns to Master Hora, the wise administrator of time. There she falls into a sleep that lasts for one year.

When she returns to the town, nobody has any time any longer. The grey men are all holding the people of "Momo`s" village at bay. The grey men want to be led to Master Hora by Momo. They want to destroy the depth of time. However, to Master Hora, are reaching only those who are going continuously slower—the slower they walk, the quicker they move forward.

Finally, Momo moves backward to get there quicker. The grey gentlemen following her are extinguished with this backward movement. Master Hora stops the time for an hour to give Momo the opportunity to find the stolen time and to give it back to the people. In this way the world gains color, vividness, and love again.

The time thieves are grey, dehumanized, mass-produced robots, like vampires, which sell the illusion that time is money and money is time, and that everything can be hoarded in bank accounts. Of course, it is a child, a girl, who liberates the world from this terrible seed of horror. "Except ye be converted, and become as little children, ye shall not enter into the kingdom of heaven," Jesus says to his disciples (Matthew 18). Jung calls this the archetype of the divine child.

How about you? Does time silence you, or are you still talking to your inner child?

Please shut your dear eyes. Imagine yourself as very small, maybe one, two, three, or four years old. How do you see yourself? Go back to the time when you lived beyond the times. Look at how boisterous, careless, pure, and free you are. Experience how you deepen and create the moment in a playful way. You are one in your interior, and you are united with the outside. Experience once again the luck in your heart, the shining of your eyes, and the alertness of your mind!

At some time you became reasonable and rational. You were functioning and made yourself perfect or simply adjusted or protested. Where did your freedom and pureness remain? There is something completely covered with dust. It whimpers in any of the far corners of your soul, left alone, with nobody to take care of it for years. Does it cry? Does it hit its head against the wall? Or is it simply staring ahead without participation?

If this is true, then please get at eye level and kneel down before this small unhappy being. Take both hands, look into its eyes, and talk in a clear, honest, and loving way. "Please, forgive me. Forgive me for not having time for you. Forgive me for my rudeness, my ignorance, my disregard, my blows and punishments, and my hard-heartedness. Forgive me for overlooking, ignoring, and tormenting you and making you worthless." Repeat these words again and again, with warmth and honesty.

Get into a deeper place inside, and open the doors to your own truthfulness. With every apology, you will see that the child will get purer, the dust will fall off, the motionlessness will loosen, and all masks that are too narrow will start to crumble.

Then come vividness, cries of fury, primal screams of life, and deep sobbing. Please take this child into your arms, embrace it, console it, and warm it up. Feel its own reawakening together with the circulating of your blood, and the throbbing of your heart. Look directly into its eyes, and say, "I love you! I love you! I love you! I love me! I love me! I love me!"

Sense the liberation of your soul, and dive into the childlike land full of magic, shining, pureness, and unspoiled joy. Enjoy the frenzy of recognizing the awakening life. Promise this child from today on that you are there for it and have time for it. Show an interest in its wishes and needs. Take your time, as this is the key to growth.

"What are its and my needs?" you will ask. First of all, they are very fundamental, and they have to do with your authenticity. Experience your feelings and sensations, realize them, and then let them flood out of your body. Then you will be free to open yourself to the wonders of this world. Dive into the room of creative freedom, develop yourself, and blossom. Your authenticity will enable you to recognize and sense your own rhythms and those of the world surrounding you. Use them for the fulfillment of your own vision.

And: Take your time!

CHRONOS

"To everything there is a season, and a time
to every purpose under the heaven.[8]

Y ou are always connected to the rhythms and cycles of your life. Rhythms characterize a periodically recurring sequence (for example, music, the year, heart rhythm, and so on). A cycle means that these rhythms are completed additionally, such as in a seasonal cycle.

Many impressions can be summarized and synchronized through the rhythm: The rhythm of activities eases the work. The rhythm of time eases the orientation in the planning of processes. Probably even the smallest electron that is revolving around its own nucleus has its own micro-rhythm.

Please shut your dear eyes. Dive into the depths of matter, and witness how everything swings rhythmically: molecules, atoms, and electrons. Visualize an ocean of streaming, pulsating energy.

The first gods and goddesses were probably the heroes of cyclic time. The Greeks knew three or four different gods of time: Chronos, the cyclical god, who later became Kronos,[9] the slaughterer Kairos, the happy moment; and Aion, eternity.

Chronos was born first. According to the myths of Orphism[10] there was chaos in the beginning. The Greek word *chaos* means the "yawning abyss" or the "gaping emptiness." The well-known philosophers Plato and Anaxagoras regard chaos as the formless, nonphysical, and unformed primary substance, the pure energy of which everything is created. Out of this dark original state arises Chronos, the creator god who fathered the silver egg from Aether, the vital principal or world soul. Phanes, the god of light, who is particularly adored in the Orphic, rose out of it. In other words, Chronos, the time, is created out of the "vacuum" field and then gives birth to space, energy, and light. We are nearly at quantum physics.

Chronos and the Egyptian time god, Horus, are connected with the various cycles of our world—the rhythm of the seasons, the rhythm of the month as a consequence of the moon phases, and the rhythm of day and night as a result of light and darkness.

As a god of light and the sky, Horus, the main god in Egyptian mythology, has a sun eye on the right and a moon eye on the left, which clearly indicate that he is cyclically looking at time. Therefore, Horus is connected not only to the male but also to the female cycle of time and can get sight of both of them.

Many old traditions regard time as an infinite dance of cycles. Huge waves of time pulsate the whole universe in different cycles, which also decisively determine our life on earth.

The Maya, whose long-term calendar went through the year 2012, knew five time cycles as a whole. The so-called big cycle, which orients itself toward the course of the earth through the Milky Way, lasts 5,125 years as a whole, the next smaller 144,000 days, then 7,200 days, 360 days, 20 days, and the smallest cycle has the fullness of 1 day. In 2012, the first big cycle, the thirteenth second cycle, and all other cycles ended at the same time. In their deep understanding of the cycles of the world, the Maya could describe up to four thousand years the time pattern of our world into the future; that would be as if we had knowledge today that would reach the year 6000!

In India, God Shiva presents with his dance the eternal energy of the creation, conservation, and destruction of the world. Shiva is also called *Maha Kala*, which means "big time," or *Kala Rudra*, which stands for "gulping time." God Vishnu is also deeply connected to the rhythms of the creation. In an eternal rhythm, Vishnu breathes in and out the creation of our world and our universe.[11]

Quantum physicists like Roger Penrose assume very profound rhythms of time; universes might disappear out of time and then bang into new existence.[12]

We are still connected here on this earth with the rhythms of our body. For this purpose, chronobiology is examining the cycles of biological unities; nearly all human beings, down to the unicellular organism, possess an inner biological clock that synchronizes with the alternation of day and night, the rhythm of the seasons, and their natural cycles. The daily inner clock is also running without daylight, as can be evidenced by plants in the darkness. People who've been locked in a bunker develop a constant wake–sleep rhythm after a while, the so-called circadian rhythm of about twenty-five hours.

Please sense your own rhythms. Your heart is hopefully regularly and coherently pumping blood through your body. This rhythm is enabling a consistent process of creation, the supply and evacuation of the needless. Of course, your breath is also following a particular rhythm and assures the regular supply with oxygen that way. Visualize your day rhythms, the course of the month, and the seasons of your life—the whole cycle that comprises your life on earth.

There is probably no function in your body that is not working in rhythms. Henrike, one of my group participants, always reported strong, suddenly occurring fears, which hit "very high," as she called it. I asked her to make a hand movement for the course of these fears. She stretched out her hands in front of her, moving in a horizontal way from left to right, then she made a horizontally stiff line running up to about the height of the navel, and suddenly she waved her whole arm at the height of the tip of her nose and then declined it to the base level. This was not a rhythmic balanced wave but a piercing rigor, which was abrupt and suddenly cut into the straight line. However, in my opinion, the problem was not only the rigor, but also the straight line.

Where do we find such lines? At the flat line. The heart is quasi pumping in sine curves, preferably well balanced, and wavy. The HeartMath Institute in California has developed a device that measures the coherence of the heartbeat. In three steps—red, blue, and green—you can get the evenness of your heartbeat, and then you receive one of the following patterns:[13]

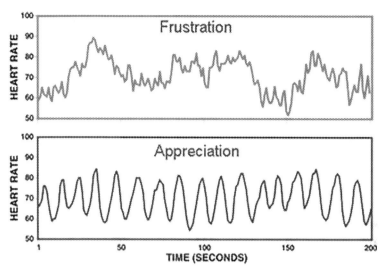

Thanks to the Institute of HeartMath for publishing the image

I hope that your heart rhythm does not resemble the first curve above. There you are not really seeing a curve, but a frizzy zigzag line of frustration and anger in the heart. The coherence is blurred. The lower swinging curve is recording a waving mood of feel-good and positive sensations.

Rhythmic movements, which can be depicted in sine curves, are the basis of coherence and health. They can occur both in a relaxed state as well as during activities. I have a device called emwave from the HeartMath Institute, and a few years ago I started to make it tempting for my little son to (as I wished in secret) come to rest more and more often. He checked it – and it permanently alarmed "red," which means his heart coherence was low. "This is a silly system. I will never do that again!" he said, and he threw the device on the desk and hurried away.

The other day he was playing with Legos in his room, sitting there dreamily on his carpet, laying brick on brick in a creative chaos. In his ear he had fixed the little device, and lo and behold, it was blinking the whole time in green! So he was in inner harmony in the middle of an apparent Lego war field!

Frieda, a middle aged woman of one of my groups, to whom I

had lent the device for some days, reported to me that it was always blinking red while she walked through the forest, where she was supposed to feel relaxed. But in the evening, when she was lying on the sofa and listened to an erotic audio, it was sparkling green! And while vacuum cleaning the house she had the same effect.

It is important to recognize our very individual rhythms, synchronize them anew, and harmonize them over the various exercises. And then when you are in coherence, you can also harmonize the tensions between fellow humans.

Please close your eyes. Imagine a beloved human being in your mind's eye. Catch sight of a pendulum at an imagined ceiling between you and the person opposite. Let it tune in the rhythm of love. Visualize a person opposite you with whom you do not have things straightened out. See the pendulum between you, and give it time to level off until the tension between you balances in a waving swing.

"Live in rhythm" old cultures demand, and even our Bible. Pete Seeger, who was well-known in the fifties for his anti-war songs, was put under pressure by his publisher to finally produce something clever and profitable. He took the Bible, one of his favorite books, into his hands and became absorbed by its texts. He nearly copied the Song of Ecclesiastes 3, adding only the last line, which is very meaningful and encouraging:[14]

> *To Everything there is a season*
> *And a time to every purpose, under Heaven*
> *A time to be born, a time to die*
> *A time to plant, a time to reap*
> *A time to kill, a time to heal*
> *A time to laugh, a time to weep*
>
> *To Everything there is a season*
> *And a time to every purpose, under Heaven*
> *A time to build up, a time to break down*

A time to dance, a time to mourn
A time to cast away stones, a time to gather stones together
To Everything there is a season
And a time to every purpose, under Heaven
A time of love, a time of hate
A time of war, a time of peace
A time you may embrace, a time to refrain from embracing
To Everything there is a season
And a time to every purpose, under Heaven
A time to gain, a time to lose
A time to rend, a time to sew
A time for love, a time for hate
A time for peace, I swear it's not too late.

However, the high season for this song came more than ten years later. As Pete emphasized, it is never too late. In the sixties it was chosen as a hit by the Byrds.

Please keep in mind that it is never too late—not for you, your healing, the change and transformation of your life, your inner peace, and of course the freedom of our world. "Paths are made by walking!" Franz Kafka already knew.[15]

Ease and lightness in life develop when we recognize the inner and outward rhythms and their synchronicity. Then Kairos might pass by—the happy, felicitous moment.

Kairos

Flickr: jinterwas - Golden times - you & me - fading into memory

Over time, Kairos became a religious/philosophical term for an opportune moment. Letting it pass unused can be disadvantageous. Over is over!

In Greek mythology, the right moment is personified by Kairos as a deity. However, it is only a minor figure at the Greek pantheon. Although a dialogue is passed on with Kairos and Posidippus of Pella, a Hellenistic poet:

Who are you?
I am Kairos who defeats everything!
Why do you tiptoe?
I, Kairos walk incessantly.
Why do you have wings at your foot?
I fly like the wind.
Why do you have a sharp knife in your hand?
To remember the people that, I am sharper than a knife.
Why does a lock fell into your forehead?
With that everybody, who is meeting me can grab me.
Why are you bald at your back of your head?
When I swept by with flying foot,
nobody can hit me from behind,
as hard as he tries.
And why did the artist create you?
As a guidance for you hikers.

The phrase "grab one's luck by the scruff of its neck" is attributed to the depiction of the god. When the opportunity is over, you cannot grasp it at the back of the head any longer. Therefore, psychology describes the fear to make decisions as Kairophobia.

Carl Gustav Jung connects Kairos to the phenomenon he calls

synchronicity. In Greek, *synchronous* means "at the same time." According to Jung, synchronicity points to correlating events that are connected to each other but are not causal (i.e., not intertwined causally). They are the cause of something, which is compatible, but fit together in a meaningful way.

Synchronicity means two events taking place simultaneously: an inner event (a dream, a vision, or a feeling) and an external event (a physical event that depicts a manifested reflection of an internal state or its equivalent). Defining a double event as synchronous requires that the inner event is happening before or exactly at the same time as the external event. Only in that way can causality be excluded.[16]

Jung referred to a young patient who proved to be "psychologically inaccessible" and with whom he remained in a persistent standstill.

> The difficulty consists in her knowing everything better. Her splendid education had given her an appropriate weapon in her hands, namely a sharpened Cartesian rationalism with a geometrically perfect concept of reality. After some fruitless efforts to reduce her rationalism with a bit more human reason I had to reduce my hope to that something unexpected and irrational may happen to her, something, that the intellectual retort she was caught in, may destroy.[17]

I can imagine vividly what a challenge this must have been for Jung. And of course, I can also imagine people who know everything better—maybe you too? I think of myself, narrowed in this tight room of reason, obviously striving for causality and might.

But Kairos was already on its way. The said patient dreamed of a golden scarab and told Jung her dream the following day. Suddenly something was knocking at his window. Jung rose, went after the sound, and discovered an insect, a *Scarabaeidae, Cetonia aurata*, a golden green rose chafer, which is very similar to the scarab. He handed it to the woman and said, "Here is your scarab." Indeed, he had forgotten the "abracadabra!" but the woman had probably heard it in her heart. This event of synchronicity bumped the desired hole into her rationalism and the ice of her intellectual resistance. The analysis could be continued successfully.

Carl Gustav Jung did not deny that each of the involved events stood in its own chain of causation. Therefore, he did not question the principle of causality but expanded it. Beyond the causality, things and appearances are correlated to each other.

The events may appear accidentally, but they are inwardly linked by meaning that develops from an effective numinous potency of an archetype. It seems as if the archetypal pattern is not only working in the individual, but also manifesting in his or her circumstances.

Anne from my group loves to be enthused. "I am pleased with the feeling of unity with the cosmos! Then I can experience how everything is connected with each other, how the inside and outside interact with each other. This touches me and it gives me power and meaning! And suddenly things happen I could only dream of, but never had considered them as possible. I feel myself in the flow and my life joins together and starts to be successful."

The so-called coincidence happens in a minimal number of occurrences. Do you agree, or have you already won a billion in the lottery? Synchronicity happens rarely. If you do not grab your luck by the scruff of its neck, it is gone forever and you are beamed back into your life of causality regarding the laws of nature. Following gravity and all other laws of nature, you are bound to earth in an unshakable way.

When you open the gates to the ocean of creation, synchronicity can develop. In this ocean everything is connected, and the waves of your life revive the ocean, just as it stimulates you.

Please close your eyes and plunge into the ocean of creation. Open all your boundaries and limits, and be the wave. Shift up and down. Sense how the ocean is forming you and moving you through the ages. Experience yourself in harmony with the flow of life. Kairos is waiting for you there. Welcome him!

KRONOS

*"Time does not fly quicker than in former
time, but we run past it quicker."*

—*George Orwell*

L ife and time are the greatest presents we have received. Do you agree?

The word "present" means "presence" and "gift". I do not know whether this effect has an etymological background or is simply presenting synchronicity. Anyway, you cannot save time, you cannot buy time, and you cannot distribute time. I can give it to you as a present. As you are reading now, you are giving your time to me. Thank you!

The Indo-Germanic root of "time" is *dai*, which means "dividing," "tearing," "separating," and "cutting up." In other words, it means something divided. Etymologically, time is related to "target" as the final point of the phase, and the isolated cell in the body, and the jail cell. Thus, the term "time" nearly implicates digitalization, with which every computer works today. The term "digitalization" means the transferring of constant size in graduated (confidential) results as a binary code.

The ancient Greeks already knew about the phenomenon of chopping up time. About 2,500 years ago they rewrote their wonderful Orphic creation myth (you read about it in the chapter titled "Chronos") and invented a new story of Chronos, whom they then called Kronos.

Kronos was born as the son of Gaia (the earth) and Uranus (the sky). Actually, this is a wonderful composition, isn't it? There was only one catch—probably the human projection has hooked in there. Above all, Uranus was not the husband but Gaia's firstborn child, whom she created without copulation via Eros in her sleep. Was this a good move with the mother and without love?

With his mother/wife, Gaia, Uranus had many descendants; however, he hated all his children. He hid them in Tartarus, in the depths of the earth. As soon as they revolted, he repeatedly pushed them with his gigantic phallus back into Gaia.

As a result, Gaia forged an enormous sickle of steel and incited her

43

sons to fight against their own cruel father (and her own son/husband). They all were shocked by this wish, but in the end the titan Kronos offered to take over this task, as Uranus was the first who had devised a disgraceful deed.

When Uranus climbed up to Gaia the next time and lay with her, Kronos castrated him with this sickle.

So Kronos took over the world domination. Fearing something similar would happen to him by his own children, Kronos killed his descendants in turn. Only his son Zeus could be saved. Today Kronos is staying somewhere on the island of bliss, in the Elysian fields at the edge of the globe.

I do not want to interpret this brutal story. I am sure that some Freudian and Jungian books can be written about it, and maybe that has already been done. I intend to explain Kronos, the "new" god of time.

He is not involved in the cycles of time any longer. On the contrary, he was the result of incest (which does not respect the cycles of generation succession) without love. Kronos destroyed the cycle of his ancestors and his descendants. Finally, he became fatherless, childless, lonesome, and separated like the phallus of his father.

Since then, this separation—the sickle—has been the symbol of death, the great reaper. It symbolically introduced the transition to the so-called patriarchal era. The former nature deities likely formed out of the texture of human forebodings and intuitions, while the undigested impulses and emotions were projected on the patriarchal rear.

On the subject of destructivity of time, there was a Top Ten hit in Germany in 1972. I have even danced to this song. It is Barry Ryan's "Time," and it might be translated like this:

> *Time does not only separate dance and dancer,*
> *Time also separates every singer and his song,*
> *As time is something, we do not belong.*

> *Time does not only separate dream and dreamer,*
> *Time also separates every poet and his word,*
> *As time runs away forward.*

Time does not only separate son and father.
Time is separating you and me one time,
As time is drawing the longest line.

When time is becoming an experience of violence, when the rhythm of death and rebirth expires, we call it "burnout." Time is getting a robber, a rapist, or a thief, as in Michael Ende's book *Momo*. The human being is becoming a machine.

Literature on this topic came on the market in the 1970s. Suffering burnout means being in a state of inner emptiness, emaciation, and physical exhaustion. It is sometimes accompanied by depersonalization and feelings of estrangement due to chronic stress. By the way, the word "chronic" also stems from *Chronos* and means "over a long period."

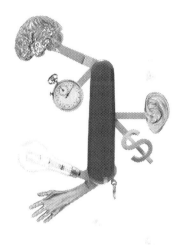

John Steinbeck, a successful American author of the last century, thought even then that the stress-related illness is an "epidemic that is caused by the hand of the clock and passed on by the appointment book." Closely linked to it are the typical medical problems that manifest, particularly in the cardiovascular area. So the heart attack is regarded as a typical expression of stress-related illness as a consequence of work pressure, sleep deficit, and a lack of relaxation and a private life.

From medicine, we know that a digitalized heart rhythm can be mortal or at least the herald of a heart attack. Even in the third century, the Chinese practitioner Wang Shu-he recognized that a variable heartbeat is a sign of health. He documented this in his work *Mai Ching (The Knowledge of Pulse Diagnosis)*. These words are attributed to him: "If the heart is as regular as the knocking of a woodpecker or the dripping of rain on the roof, the patient will die within four days." I've read that "digitalized rhythms in discos can harm liver complaints while drum rhythms – beating in the same rhythms – can have a healing influence."

The opposite of burnout (hectic, hurry, or senseless restlessness) is "deceleration." The term was created at the end of the 1970s too. It means the rediscovery of slowness via the slowing down of psychological, economical, ecological, and social processes, a break in this world that accelerates.

I would like to introduce you to another break. Would you like to dive with me into your own creativity and float in a flow? There you meet your very self. There you can deepen and fulfill time. In this abundance, you return home. "How do I get there?" you might ask.

Do you know Leonard Cohen's song "Anthem"? He says, "There is a crack in everything, that's where the light comes in."

Please close your eyes. Imagine a crack that cuts time, as well as humanity, and that rips our lives apart. Visualize the cut in your head and in your heart. It separates your head from your heart. Feel the pain, sorrow, and rage of centuries of people who felt torn apart, loosened out of their center, and forced away from their authenticity. They abandoned their soul. Breathe out, scream, and cry. Breathe out, scream, and cry. Breathe out, scream, and cry. After releasing all the built-up oppression and held-back emotions, relax and tune back into your authentic center. It is all over now. These times have passed.

Breathe in through your heart. Breathe in through the crack. With every breath, dive deeper and deeper into this hole in your heart. Watch. Do you see the small spark of light? Dive deeper and deeper, and watch how you come closer and closer to the flame of your life. See how it grows, increases, and rises—a new sun, a new morning, a new day. After all the time behind fortification walls and veils, you have come back to your inner light. The pain is the way. The sorrow is the gate. The rage is the opener. Step into the light. You are welcome. It is a new time. This time it is your life.

With our imaginations, we do not stop Kronos. No, we delightfully pass him by. We just switch the track to our land of magic, our fantasy kingdom, the light inside. We can imagine while waiting at the traffic light; we can imagine even while taking a boring seminar or while baking bread. At the red light we start to have time for ourselves. Thank traffic for the rest. We interpret the red light as a stop—a stop of Kronos—and then we fly straight to our magic kingdom to heal. In a boring seminar, we take the humdrum speech as a lullaby and dream away in our visions, and while baking bread we connect with the nourishing energies of the earth. We take the world around us as a gateway to our creativity. We take the crack in our hearts as the entrance to our true self. We take the cry of Kronos as an impulse for healing.

AEON

"The flowing Now makes the time, the standing Now makes the eternity."[18]
— *Anicius Boethius.*

For the sake of completeness, I will talk to you about *Aeon*, or *Aion*, an ancient philosophical and religious term that describes the embodied world time or eternity. In Greek literature, *Aeon* means "life" or "lifetime." However, it remains unclear if Aeon was treated as more than a god or as a personified concept of eternity and deity.

In Greek philosophy, Aeon is first mentioned by Heraclitus as a boy who is moving gaming pieces forward and backward. Does the game indicate the succession of cyclical periods of time? When the gaming pieces are positioned, a new game, a new cycle, starts. However, Plato uses the term "Aion" anticyclical as a linear time sequence. Aristoteles describes eternity as *telos* ("completion")—not only of the human being but also of the whole universe. And the Bible presents a certain ambiguity. When you pray "from now until eternity," eternity is limited by the "now." Is it still eternity then?

So the Greek Aeon received two meanings in the course of time— let us say a millionth of eternity. Aeon means "age" (i.e., a limited period of time) and "eternity" (i.e., an unlimited time).

Even in the mythological "dreamtime" of Australian natives, the aborigines depict an eternal world, without space and time, from which the real world is born in an incessant process of creation. This dreamtime does not have anything to do with the dreams in sleep, but with the dreaming powers in the cosmos, from which our so-called everyday reality comes into being. According to the imagination of the aborigines, well-informed persons can get in contact with the dreamtime and its figures via certain rituals and ceremonies at any time, particularly at holy locations. Since the populating of Australia forty thousand years ago, people started to report about the creation of the world in dreamtime legends, which were orally handed down. However, the dreamtime is not an unchangeable moral authority; it "learns" from the experience of the world beyond. There is nothing that is not connected to the dreamtime. In the imagination of the aborigines, a "dreaming landscape" is the embodiment of mystic realities, which is hard to explain in words.

"Eternity can be influenced via events in time," said David Bohm,[19] a quantum physicist who lived in the past century. He tried to bridge the latest research with the core statements of the mystics, particularly Krishnamurti. Therefore, he developed a revolutionary view of consciousness. Besides the three-dimensional world of the objects in space and time, Bohm assumed that there was an inner dimension underlying the appearances, in which all realities and possibilities were included in space- and timelessness. He called it the "implicit order." There the connecting of moments occurs, which we call time. Matter and consciousness are building an inseparable unity in these dimensions.

Again we arrive at our eternal foaming ocean of creation, which is quasi-eternal itself, but whose white crests are extending widely into the world of matter. Just as timelessness is hidden in the depth of time, eternity is slumbering on the ground of this ocean. Time structures this eternal ocean in an abundance that we can experience and be a part of. "As my soul asked what eternity does with the desires we gathered, it answered: I am eternity!" wrote Khalil Gibran.[20]

Why is all this important for self-healing in everyday life, where even natural scientists and philosophers are not on the same page? We appear to branch off the topic. However, on our inner journeys we are always diving into what we call eternity. The pictures take away our souls' fear of change, transformation, and dissolution. They introduce us to a grandeur that connects us to everything.

Then we breathe in eternity in the form of Whitney Houston's international hit "One Moment in Time:"

Give me one moment in time
When I am more than I thought I could be
When all my dreams are a heartbeat away
and the answer is all up to me
And in that moment of time
I will feel eternity.

Clock Time

"Time is what you read from the clock."
—*Albert Einstein*

Yesterday I looked for a new clock at the clockmaker's, as my old clock got wet and did not function any longer. There are so many angular clocks. Can you imagine angular time? Many clocks have digital displays. Our digitalized age includes only a few round clocks. In former times, the sundials symbolized the cycle of time. With digital clocks, time continues to progress without rhythm. Is time hurrying away from itself?

For Heraclitus, time was the river of life, the continuous change. For Aristoteles, it was inseparably connected to change too. According to Sir Isaac Newton, absolute, true, and mathematical time flows uniformly and without relation to any outer object. We imagine it still like that: There is an objective and absolute atomic clock hanging somewhere outside the universe, and it ticks to itself, probably not on a round hand, but continuously processing in figures.

Physics maintained the worldview until Albert Einstein worded the special theory of relativity in 1905. What was radically new was the statement that time does not exist independent from events and not independent from space, but rather it is part of the universe as a fourth dimension, tightly embraced in a space-time. Time and space are also always two aspects of the same stuff, interweaved in a space-time continuum that has developed since the big bang. John Wheeler, Einstein's contemporary who was a bit younger, explained, "Time is what prevents everything from happening at once."[21]

Time describes the sequence of events. In contrast to other physical values, it has a clear, irreversible direction. According to the physical principles of thermodynamics, time can be considered the increase of entropy (i.e., the disorder in a system). From a philosophical point of view, time describes the progress of the presence coming from the past, leading into the future. Therefore, the term "presence" can only be defined as one single point, while other points of space-time, which are laying in the past or in the future, can be regarded as "separated like space."

The most prominent quality of time is the fact that there always seems to be a current we call presence, which moves incessantly from the past to the future. This phenomenon is also called the flow of time.

However, the apparent flowing of time is regarded by most physicists and philosophers as a purely subjective phenomenon or even as an illusion. Invalid is our daily idea that there is an authority that is independent from the person in the form of a cosmic clock, which determines the point of time we all experience together in this moment and which creates the presence to an objective that connects us all.

In Albert Einstein's developed theory of relativity, data of space and time are not universally valid order structures any longer, but they are always related relatively to the observers. In comparison to the resting state in the direction of movement, objects prove themselves as shortened and moved clocks as slowed down. However, the uniformly moved observers can take the view that they are at a standstill, and these observations are mutual (i.e., two observers who are approaching one another see that the clock of the prevailing other person is moving slower).[22] Moreover, the presence of masses influences the course of time so that it goes by at different speeds in various locations on the gravitational field.

In the general theory of relativity, time is not necessarily unlimited. Many physicists assume that the big bang is not only the beginning of the existence of matter, but also the start of space and time. According to Stephen Hawking, there was no point of time a second before the big bang, no more than a point on the earth that lays one kilometer north of the North Pole. Thus, is time a ball? Many questions have arisen concerning the phenomenon of time.

Anyway, I will not confuse you here any longer, but I will tempt you to turn to the next chapter about time, with a joke from Einstein: "If you sit two hours together with a girl, you think that it was a minute. However, if you sit a minute on a hot oven you think it was two hours. That is relativity."

Subjectivity of Time

"As a child in luck and sorrow the time crept slowly. As a youth proud and bold it went for a walk. As a mature man I sometimes saw it rushing terribly." ... *goes the inscription of a German bell.*[23]

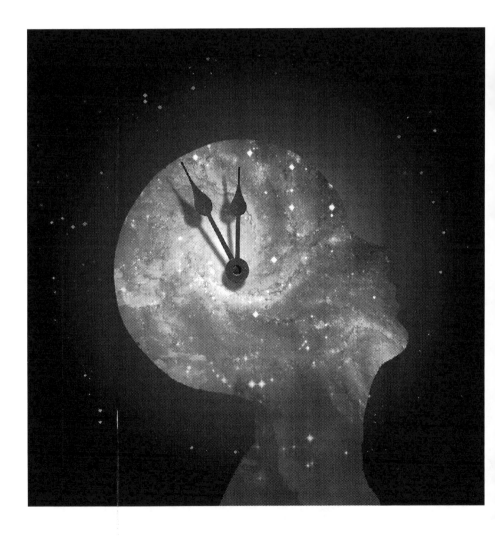

Between the subjectively perceived time and the time that can be measured objectively, there often is a significant difference. The perception of time depends on how old you are or how old you feel and what happens in the time.

An eventful period of time appears often too short and passes quickly, while uneventful periods of time are sometimes terribly long. Paradoxically, in retrospect, you sense it in reverse order. In eventful times you have stored a lot of information so that this period appears to be long. In reverse order, uneventful times appear to be short, as there is hardly anything substantial about them that was adhered to in your brain.

The subjective simultaneity has to be taken with a grain of salt. The threshold, when two events can be recognized as separate, depends on the prevailing sense organ. For human beings, optical impressions have to be further apart chronologically than acoustic perceptions to notice them seperatedly. The threshold from which the sequence of two stimulations can be distinguished depends on the kind of perception and always orients to the slowest stimulation transfer. Moreover, the stimulus of the present is indicated by a three-second period.

So what do you think time is? Is it the course of events through space? Is it your inner time? Where is it? We do not see it, hear it, or smell it. There is only the presence. With every passing second we design our presence and create our future. Every second puts us in front of a guide sign of our destiny, and we can always choose from the field of infinite possibilities. Every second of your life—with all its thoughts, actions, and feelings—decides your whole future and ultimately the future of mankind.

In every second you have infinite possibilities. In every hour eternity slumbers. Choose what is fitting for you. Again, there are many possibilities. We have reached the field of possibilities, the real potential, the seed of our possible future. However, it seems that time does not exist there yet.

Timelessness

"The moment is a-temporal."
—*David Bohm*

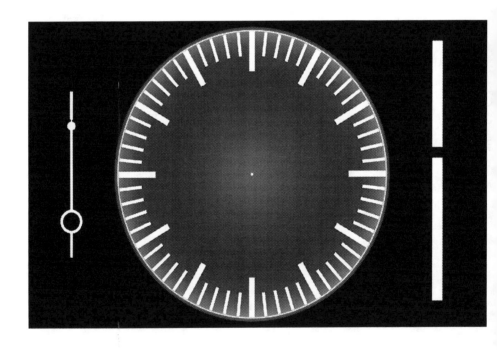

While we are considering the concept of eternity more philosophically and also theologically, quantum physicists have investigated "spaces" of time, as well as timelessness.

Time probably started about thirteen or even fourteen billion years ago in a tremendous explosion of highly intensive radiation. Within a quintillion of a second—this is a figure with thirty zeros—space blew out from an undefinable, infinite little point that physicists call "singularity." The energy density was unimaginably high, the temperature boiling hot, and the speed very fast. At the same time, the space was formed and with it the direction of the time arrow. Astrophysicists call the starting point at which this time arrow was quasi shot down "Planck time." It defines the earliest possible state of the world, how it might have been very shortly after the big bang. First and foremost, it formed the border of the classic description of space and time. Everything that might have happened before the Planck time for the first time goes beyond the scope of Einstein's theory of relativity, as it does not describe the time before.

Maybe other universes existed before. Maybe even several universes were thrown into space. Maybe there was nothing or everything. Who knows?

The Planck time, named after the famous German physicist Max Planck, describes the smallest possible time interval, which is valid for the well-known laws of physics. It results from the time that requires light to do a Planck length. In smaller time intervals, time probably loses its familiar attitudes as a continuum. It would quantize (i.e., time would run below the Planck time in discreet jumps). In the current physical laws, every object that goes through a process in less than a Planck time collapses into a black hole. Some theoretical physicists even assume that time will become discontinuous. In the same way matter consists of atoms, the second can assemble out of present granules that follow one another, if we only get deep enough into its interior.

In 1967, the second was officially cut into pieces. Scientists of about forty nations made the radical decision in Paris that the rotation of the earth should not determine the rhythm of the world but the atom. The second is defined as 9,192,631,770 times the cycle duration of a resonance frequency of a cesium atom. This is more precise than the rotation of the earth, which fluctuates within a millionth of a second due to the tides. Cesium atoms are always functioning in the same way, whether at your home, at my home, on earth, or in the universe.

An eyelid movement lasts only a few milliseconds (a thousandth of a second), and a flash of lightning several microseconds (a millionth of a second). Electrons are dashing around the nucleus with a speed of one million kilometers per hour. A femtosecond is a billionth of a second. If our perception was fast enough, we would see the electromagnetic field of light swing like the pendulum of a cuckoo clock.

But it is a long way until we get there. Currently physicists have the attosecond in their sights; it starts with eighteen digits after the comma and establishes the atto-physics. Ferenc Krausz, a physicist at the Max Planck Institute in Munich, has investigated with laser light the tiniest time intervals of quantum time. These time intervals are really little. An attosecond corresponds, for example, to a trillionth part of a second or a billionth of billionth part of a second. Molecules dance in step in attoseconds. In this inconceivable period of time, scientists have discovered an area in which no time exists, in which the distance between one event and the next does not have a meaning and does not make sense. The fascinating result is that below this time limit, no movement and no change is measurable. It somehow disappears or dissolves, and there is a standstill and timelessness. For a massless part like a photon, time does not seem to pass.

When I descend into smaller and smaller time units, I come across the phenomenon of timelessness, in the same way as if I find energy on the bottom of matter. That means that very deep down there and very high above or around us or even within us, energy and timelessness are slumbering. On the bottom of our ocean of creation rests timeless potentiality.

Some quantum physicists imagine quantum reality as timeless. Maybe the basic description of the universe should be radically timeless.

The content of this book as a whole is present for you at the same time. It's quasi-timeless and is only coming through the connection of you and your reading into the illusion of a chronology. Maybe a quantum event might come into being out of seemingly nothing in a fundamentally timeless world. When we count back, it is getting smaller and smaller, until it dives into a timeless "fog" without dynamic. The origin of all time seems to be timelessness. Is it really possible that time is only an illusion?

"What you name the ghost of the times is at root our own mind in which the times are reflecting themselves," wrote Goethe two hundred years ago.

Do you think it is possible that the events of the world are saved at the same time on a kind of cosmic DVD, and even our consciousness brings everything into a chronological order?

What do you think about Khalil Gibran's idea that time is the observer that brings the distance between it and what it is creating? At the same time, he warns: Of time you would make a stream upon whose bank you would sit and watch its flowing. Yet the timeless in you is aware of life's timelessness.[25]

Please shut your dear eyes again, and breathe in and out. Let yourself fall into the center of yourself. Do you feel the time? When you have reached inside of yourself, are you then in the time? Or outside? Or in your own time? Or beyond time?

Carl Gustav Jung regarded the psyche as timeless. For the unconscious psyche, space and time seem to be relative (i.e., the knowledge is beyond a spatiotemporal continuum in which space and time are no longer time).[26] Maybe you can sense, like Krishnamurti[27] or even Meister Eckhart[28] and the wise men before you, that time does not exist in the center of you. There you can discover the spaceless room of your self and your fantasy.

Stephen Hawking, a famous quantum physicist, introduced the term "imaginary time.". On the horizontal axis the calendar is presented backward and forward, and on the vertical axis is the imaginary time with all its possibilities.

Maybe we are weaving our life there, in a kind of dreamtime, with our magic inner journeys, imagination, and fantasy.

Now

"Open your feast and let go! Then there is infinite much space, open, inviting, pleasant."
—*Gendun Rinpoche*

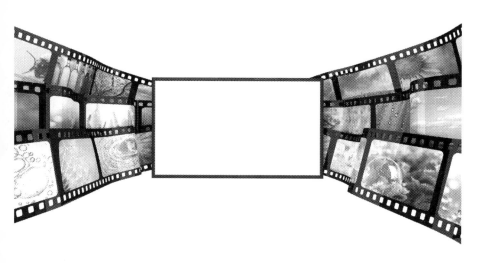

Please look at your life for a moment, from your birth until today. Was it not a series of countless present moments? As soon as you think about the past, this also happens in the present, and likewise the visions of your future are happening in the present. There really is only the present, as the present is always there. It might be called the gateway to eternity.

The wise men of various traditions have always given the present a spiritual and healing meaning. The Sufi called themselves the "children of presence." The Zen masters taught the power of the presence. The Bible says, "Therefore do not worry about tomorrow, for tomorrow will worry about itself," and, "No man, having put his hand to the plough, and looking back, is fit for the kingdom of God." We are also remembering Lot's woman who turns to a pillar of salt when she looks back. An immovability develops when we do not flow with the presence, when we are entranced and paralyzed by our past. So even the wise men affirmed the power of now:

> Take care for this day, as it is your life – the life of all lives.
> In its short course lies all its reality and truth of
> being, the joy of growing, the greatness of action,
> the magnificence of power.
> As yesterday is nothing but a dream
> and tomorrow is only a vision.
> However, today wants to be lived in the right way,
> It turns every yesterday into a dream full of joy
> and every tomorrow into a vision of hope.
> Therefore, take very good care of this day.[29]

Your life from birth until today has been a succession of uncountable presence. Now you are reading these lines—what kind of time do you have? Do not look at the clock, but instead look inside of you, as it is always present. Eckhart Tolle, specialist of the present moment through his book *The Power of Now*, experienced the omnipresence of the presence when he contemplated suicide in a deep crisis. He continuously expressed, "I cannot live with myself any longer," until his mind revealed the paradox of the "I" split. His mind was caught in a hamster wheel and … abracadabra! Once he was standing still, only listening to his thoughts and silence, he experienced bliss.

Eckhart Tolle thinks that our Western identification with the mind is the substantial blockade that prevents enlightenment. To identify the mind means to live between memory and expectation. The mind creates a veil between I and the self, between I and world, between I and nature, and between I and God. It is an illusion of separation. As a dog likes to chew on a bone, the mind gets its teeth into problems that are his feed. With it, it destroys joy, peace, curiosity, enthusiasm, freshness, and astonishment. It is a master of maintaining the past. Most times our thinking is not only in vain; it is also harmful. The mind is incessantly busy comparing the present moment with the past and the future. The vivid and creative potential of being, which cannot be separated from the now, is covered by the mind.[30] The presence is always there, so why resist, as it is everything we have? "Gain the moment's friendship!" Eckhart Tolle demands.[31]

Please close your dear eyes. Focus your attention on your mind, which uses its energy for letting the poor hamster run on its wheel infinitely. It is always the same prospect. Now open the cage, and set the poor little animal on a green spring meadow. Let it lollop off. If you don't want to be alone - take a parrot. Annika, a young woman, did it that way. At least she could speak with the parrot. It permanently reflected her one-sidedness. May be then you get conscious of your mind's dialogues, Let the parrot be free too. It is better to use your energy to wave new networks, which expand, deepen, increase, and center the presence in your mind.

Everything is in the presence and in every moment. And this presence is everything we have, and in this presence we have everything. This presence exists. Think about the past; it is an act of the presence. Think of the future; it is an act of the presence. All signs of a past exist only in the presence, and every reason to believe in the future exists only in the presence too. When the real past occurred, it was not the past but the presence, and when the real future is there, it will not be the future but the presence. The only time we can ever experience is the present moment, with its memories and expectancies, its hopes and fears, its imprints and desires. Fill and fulfill it!

The eternal presence is the room in which your whole life is played out. It is the only force that is permanent, even if it is always changing in its expression. Life is happening in the presence. Presence is the key to freedom.

Please shut your dear eyes. Breathe out fears of the past. Breathe out fears of the future. Breathe out. Descend with every breath on the golden stair of your heart until you reach the gate on which stands "your true self". Open the gate. Enter it. Ask the wisdom of yourself the question, "Who am I beyond fears of the past and fears of the future? Who am I beyond yesterday and tomorrow?" Listen to the answer.

Johannes of my groups received the wonderful answer, "Beyond yesterday and tomorrow you are pure, clear, and free—newborn!" Margarethe heard, "You are the grace of letting go and the breath of fullness!" Ricarda heard, "You are a wide room of thankfulness. Listen to your own inner wisdom!"

There are infinite keys to this location that is called presence—awareness exercises, meditations, pauses, breathing, imaginations, and many more. The presence is a guesthouse. The human existence is a guesthouse.

This being human is a guest house.
Every morning a new arrival.
A joy, a depression, a meanness,
some momentary awareness comes
as an unexpected visitor.

Welcome and entertain them all!
Even if they are a crowd of sorrows,
who violently sweep your house
empty of its furniture,
still, treat each guest honorably.
He may be clearing you out
for some new delight.
The dark thought, the shame, the malice.
meet them at the door laughing and invite them in.
Be grateful for whatever comes.
because each has been sent
as a guide from beyond.[32]

"This is easier said than done," you might want to shout to me. "How shall I accept the nastiness of my neighbors, the loss of my parents, the crisis in the office, and my physical illness? It is rather the fear that will kill me yet!"[33]

It is true that I want to challenge you with every line. Enter this room of acceptance and the creation of infinite possibilities, as timelessness, eternity, rhythmic time, or simply silence. Here and now you can imagine the richness of life as a wonderful garden. Ride on the waves of your breath. Bathe in light and blessed eternity, or dissolve into a room of emptiness. Now is a gateway into the waves of our ocean of creation, and this infinite part inside you, which transpersonal psychology calls consciousness, is creating your life.

What is the most beautiful moment of your life? Of course, now! Dance with Elvis Presley: "It's Now or Never"!

Time Out

"The break also belongs to rhythm."
—Stefan Zweig

Instructions for Everyday Practice

"Nourish the exercise and it starts to nourish you."
—*Chameli Ardagh*[34]

Everyday occurrences are brilliant for creating your life in an efficient and simple way. Your brain enjoys habits, and every cell is informed and feels safe. However, we have learned a routine that restricts, limits, and harms us sometimes, despite helping us in lightness. "Bad" habits include not only smoking cigarettes and drinking alcohol, but also those everyday processes and reactions that move us away from ourselves (for example, when you discharge your duties in a compulsive way despite tiredness, when you smile although your body is shedding tears, when you get a stomachache despite expressing your fury, and when you distract yourself with superficialities despite experiencing your own depth). There you will find the foundation of your being.

Techniques and Tools

Stop.

No matter how, leave the tiring route of everyday life again and again. The only important thing is that the routine of everyday life will be broken in two. In a pinch, reset a clock, or program your mobile. Stop your automatisms every few hours in a conscious way.

When you live next to a church and the bell rings, think of yourself. Margot from my groups, neither an owner of a mobile nor the neighbor of a church, has put small bells everywhere. When she opens a door, they ring. When she walks along, she touches them so that they ring joyfully. And she takes this ringing as a signal to stop her prevailing action and enable a backpedaling.

Look inside.

Take a break. Get conscious of the moment now. What do you sense, feel, experience? In order to really get yourself into it, shut your eyes. Find a loving relation to every part of your body. When attention is pouring into you, it can relax and metabolize better. Fill it up with more energy. Look inside means to focus on yourself, your current truthfulness, and your authenticity, and give yourself more space and time.

Exhale.

If you are stressed, you probably often hold your breath, or you start to breathe flatter unconsciously. So take your time to breathe out first, to give your body space to draw a breath, and to widen.

Please shut your dear eyes. Breathe out. Breathe out the exertion, the perfection, the pressure to perform, or the boredom of an automated life. Breathe out whatever rises to the surface of your consciousness. Let the seemingly unpleasant feelings take up room until they disappear in the infinites of this world. Free yourself from everyday worries, from functioning and estrangement. Take off all your armor, your roles, and your shells, like clothes that have gotten too narrow and that you have grown out of.

Breathe through your heart.

If your body is in harmony, several systems cooperate better together. Your heart is the strongest vibration generator; therefore, it can pull the other body systems into its rhythm. With the sensation of love and esteem, the mind can influence your heart frequency and generate a coherence that is perceived by every cell.

Visualize how your steady heartbeat streams through your whole body and relaxes. Observe how you throw a stone into the quiet water and it spreads equally round wavy patterns. Imagine your heart pulsates like that. Experience peace and well-being in your body. Then imagine connecting your brain and your heart with silver threads so that both are cooperating well.[35]
You can also breathe in through your heart chakra, and imagine there is

a nose that breathes the air in and out. Or imagine a flower or blossom that opens and shuts. Take the lotus blossom and let negativity drip off.

Sense yourself.

Find your "self." With every breath you go deeper and deeper into your swinging center. Sense your very own self in a genuine, pure, and clear way. Enjoy the clearness of awakening, the openness, and the curiosity for what is happening with you right now.

Align.

In the middle of yourself you will find the silence to steer your life. Where will you go if not back into your everyday routine? Decide for yourself! Connect with your creativity and the source of life. Bathe in it, dance in it, and bubble in it. Then let yourself fertilize from the source of life, and swim!

Before all exercises, focus your tender attention inside, freeing yourself from all pent-up emotions while giving them space-time until they exhaust and express themselves fully. Then they can dissolve. When you are empty from them, you can find yourself. In your center of silence, you can connect with your source of life and align with a new beginning in the best way. There you can imagine everything possible (and also everything impossible) in a free and wild way.

Imagine.

What does imagination mean? I have described it in detail in my book *Das Buch der Selbstheilung ("The Book of Self-Healing")*. The term comes from the Latin word *imago*, which means "picture," "portrait," "image," "illusion," "idea," and "allegory." As a verb it means "to imagine," "to illustrate something," and "to design a picture of something."

The sequence of pictures is a consequence of the ability to imagine, which is available to every human being from childhood on. Fantasy lives in imagination. However, it expands and enlightens it with the dimension of freedom. I can fantasize about everything. There are no limits, as I am deeply connected to the ocean of creation.

Imagination is old. Besides the laying on of hands, it is probably one of the oldest methods to change consciousness, the brain, and the body.

Imagination is a basic activity in successful self-healing. Consciousness will be changed when it is stimulated to leave tracks, which are stuck.

The pre-linguistic imagination makes use of special nerve tracts for the transfer of information. With pre-verbal imagination, the inner pictures directly communicate with the tissue and directly effect a change concerning behavior that can be checked physiologically and biochemically.

According to today's prevailing insights, the language of the pictures is primarily located in the right half of the brain and is directly connected to the sensory impressions of the body. When I try to let you imagine I have to use language. I have to choose a language that stimulates your inner pictures.

The following imaginations might always stimulate you: the crown, the wings, the smile, the wand. The imagined crown brings your body into an upright position, the spinal column swings slightly, and your soul shifts into a position of dignity. The wings help you to widen your thorax and remind your soul of its ability to fly … to Fantasia, the land of possibility. The smile suggests to your body the joys of life that it directly transforms into a cascade of feel-good hormones. You can swing the wand to change your inner pictures. Abracadabra!

As soon as you shut your eyes you can dive into your inner imagery. When you do this regularly, exercises will be created.

Exercise.

Most of the time in these exercises I give you inner pictures you can imagine, which have a direct influence on the biochemistry of your body, your hormonal balance, your heartbeat, your breath, your muscle tension, and many other things. In the broadest sense, you are steering not only your body but also your destiny with every single thought. "Know thyself: Healthy is whoever has healing thoughts" is my modern translation of the inscription on the temples of Asclepius two thousand years ago. This truth is confirmed more and more in today's neuropsychological research.

The exercises described here are ways to make your everyday life more fulfilled, lighter, and more joyful. Some of them might be known to you from other systems, though many of them are probably strange to you. Try them, learn something new, take what you need, and practice what you require for a fulfilled life. Exercise, exercise, exercise, and that way the exercises will turn into habits, and the habits will gift you with a new life. You are creating yourself according to your very own wishes, desires, and visions.

Finally, I have prepared exercises to fit with the rituals of your everyday life. Therefore, you can change your everyday routine into healing rituals, thereby creating new automatisms that serve your health and its fulfillment. Held by rituals, your life can be easier, and old things can be let off. It will be easier to learn new things. The new exercises will become a daily healing habit, and you will be a liberated and creative personality. Then you will serve yourself and your loved ones equally.

Internalize.

The exercises directly lead you into salutary thoughts and pictures. You can internalize them, and they can develop their healing power when they get under your skin. That means that pictures and also all the other exercises have to evoke a resonance within you, a feeling of touch, a sense of tingling, streaming, and pulsating. Then the mental picture will turn into the body's own experience, which can sometimes touch you as deeply as "real" experiences. Whenever you are enthused your neuropsychology constructs new networks.

Create a posture of enthused learning, an enthusiasm for yourself, your life, your development, your unfolding, and your healing. You are worth pausing, experiencing yourself, sensing yourself, and orienting anew. You are born for a vivid, fulfilled, and healing life. And you are born to accept a challenge and learn new ways. You are on your way to discover deep powers within you and to experience the deep wonder of yourself. What a chance!

Your wonderful body also works even if your will is lame. For example, you only need to smile for a while—even if you are not really in the mood—and *whoosh*, your brilliant body produces so-called happiness hormones, which bring you the joy that you desire. Laughing requires an effort of only thirteen muscles, whereas a contrite grimace requires a threefold effort.

If even thirteen muscles are too exhausting for you, then take package tape and stick it at the corners of your mouth for a while. You might laugh skeptically now. Frieda from my groups did this in order to relieve her depression, and it worked wonderfully. She had to laugh heartily about herself. The depressive automatism was broken in two with this exercise.

Yes, laughing helps. Just start with sounds that are perhaps artificial in the beginning, get into it softly (as in a cheering), and experience how you are suddenly giggling, gaggling, bubbling, and chuckling. After a few minutes your body is probably more relaxed, and your mind is more alert.

Otherwise, jump like a child with excited anticipation. This elicits the happy hormones. Long for the fulfillment of your dreams, as you did when you were seventeen. Let it grow into the sky of your love for yourself.

You might have some of your own ideas to exercise an enthused posture and free will that concentrates on your fulfilled and healthy life.

FROM YOUR DAILY ROUTINE TO YOUR HEALING RITUAL

"The way is the goal."

—Confucius

Pink can encourage you on your way to transform your life:

Gotta get up and try, and try, and try
You gotta get up and try, and try, and try.

For us "routine" means an ability we have won by exercises and experiences. The term is a French word and means in its derivation "route," the habit of staying in the paved ways, a kind of being well-informed about the ways.[36]

Routine happens if an action, a feeling, or a thought is repeated often and becomes a habit, which means it becomes a posture or an action that automatically proceeds without our control. Our brain likes habits. It even releases endogenous chemical messengers if its actions are automatic, and it is allowed to act in an experienced way. Routine minimizes the neuronal expenditure and with it the energy for the metabolism too.

Do you recognize some of your daily routines?

Usual habits proceed in a secure, precise, and quick way (in contrast to new and unfamiliar tasks). For that purpose, the working memory in the cerebral cortex has to be switched on to what requires more time and energy. Those who learn to drive a car create new networks for unusual behavior. The cerebral cortex works with centers, which are responsible for unconscious, automated actions and reflexes (for example, the cerebellum or the basal ganglia). They control more than 90 percent of our everyday routines. Bit by bit these new networks get more effective and quicker. With growing automation, the activity shifts from the cerebral cortex into the cerebellum and the basal ganglia. Learned habits now proceed automatically (i.e., without conscious control).

Besides saving work for the brain, routine has another advantage; many behavior habits include waking up, going to bed, and dining. Basic physical needs, such as hunger and tiredness, always return; therefore, they lead to regularity in everyday life. A structured day with the same or similar processes offers security and saves time and energy for new information and requirements, which have to be managed.

Routine provides safety and basic trust. Until the age of ten years, routine actions can be conditioned very well.

We have learned a lot of these routines, and we have internalized the doctrine that started in our early years. So we've used a minimal percentage of our brain by conscious decisions. The predominant rest is done by our cerebellum without our help.

Despite all neuronal ingenuity, routine also has a drawback, which causes in the extreme case immovability up to a pure functioning. "I became a mother machine," complains Martha from my groups, for example. We degenerate daily to an insufficient substitute for a machine, which does not require any sleep and can work twenty-four hours a day.

Carl Gustav Jung realized that early.

"Conventions are namely soulless mechanisms, which can never do more than to register the routine

79

of life. However, the creative life is always beyond the convention. This is the reason why, in case the mere routine of life in the form of traditional conventions, a destructive breakout of the creative vigors has to follow... Whoever can say yes to the power of his or her inner life will become a great personality. So the great personality works in a socially solving, releasing, transforming, and healing way. Thus the birth of an own personality has a healing effect on the individual. It is as if a river which is losing in marshy branches is suddenly discovering its streambed. Or like a stone which is lifted and under which a germinating seed was lying. So the shoot can now start its natural growth. The voice inside is the voice of a fuller life, a wider, extensive consciousness.[37]

Finally, diseases can come into being when we orient too rigidly outwardly and ignore the inner vigors of the self. The way to self-healing is no way into normalcy, but rather individuality. Self-healing is no process of adjustment, but rather of development. Self-healing does not lead into isolation, but rather opens for your own interior and that of the world. From a quantum physical point of view, the self is a force field, a hologram. We might imagine it as a permanently changing, complex, informed field of life, which is open and centered simultaneously.

We often learn to concentrate on being "good," hardworking, and functioning. These are the massively carved doctrines and attitudes that evoke automatisms in our brains. These, as modern neuroscience confirms, are the habit networks, which are now in the basal ganglias and the cerebellums, and aren't directly exposed to conscious will. Thus, routines and habits are quite immunized against changes.

But there is a timescale between irritant and reaction. We have the power to choose our reaction. We have the chance to develop our inner freedom.

Please close your dear eyes. Look inside. What do you experience in this moment? How do you sense yourself? Are you entangled in routine, or are you quite spontaneous, free, and open? Where do you really want to go to?

With a lot of alertness, attention, consciousness, exercises, and cheerful enthusiasm, new processes can become habits. Studies show they require about two months of daily exercises for complex changes, such as a new sport routine.[38] Please take your time in the next months for the development and stabilization of healing rituals so that they can strike roots.

At the beginning of her self-healing activity in the group, Andrea blamed me (admittedly in a loving way). "Alexandra, you brainwash us." This expression irritated me in the beginning. I wanted to defend myself. After a while, the following picture took shape: the laundered, cleaned brain.

Please open your skullcap, and air your brain. Open your parting chakra, and release inconvenient and rigid automatisms. Watch how they escape over your head as dulled clouds. Clean and wash away the incrustation. Massage every nerve fiber until they all can swing freely and link together anew in an enthusiastic way—for a new composition of your fulfillment. Just like that.

Dr. Joe Dispenza says in his book, *Breaking the Habit of Being Yourself: How to Lose Your Mind and Create a New One*, it takes four weeks for a normal personality to be changed. He suggests more or less the following process: In the first week, you learn the induction, the trance for achieving a state of coherent brain waves. The second week's topic is the life review and to occupying oneself with emotions, as well as emotional blockades. The third week is dedicated to releasing the past and opening for a new attitude. The fourth week serves for the creation of a new posture and its practice in life. In the time afterward: live your new reality![39]

In this book we do not plan certain topics; we seize on the symbolism of day and night and anchor our new learning in the natural rhythms. Everyday life is marked by recurring patterns of work and trips to work, consuming (shopping and eating), free time, personal hygiene, social and cultural activities, doctor visits, and sleep. The everyday life is contrasted by bank holidays, feast days, or vacations.

If we want to change the "everyday" into an "ever day," we might need to stop turning the time and whirl ourselves.

You can change every activity of the day into a ritual of healing. You can recharge each of these activities with magic, dignity, and decision. In Latin, *ritus* means above all a religious rule or ceremony. In a figurative sense, it also means a tradition or a custom.

Rituals nourish our life, as they offer us identity, a consecrated time, and a consecrated place by creating identification marks that are our homeland, and, as Anselm Grün describes it, they "open the heaven over our life."[40]

There are cultures on this earth whose routines are predominantly nourished by rituals. The morning might start with a purification ritual. Every ablution becomes a spiritual act of purification. Every step—yes, every breath—is deeply woven in unity as an umbilical cord that nourishes healing and health. So the whole life becomes an ode to creation, a place of manifestation and permanent metamorphosis of creative energy in a celebration of being.

"You gotta get up and try, and try, and try."

Yes, but what? Well, life! And when do we start? At midnight. Then all the unconscious spirits wake up for a new attitude. With this turning point of the days, you can quasi change your life. "There are two ways to live your life: Either that nothing is a miracle or that everything is one. I believe in the latter," Albert Einstein recognized. How do you decide?

MIDNIGHT

*"Shoot for the moon. Even if you miss,
you'll land among the stars."*

—Lee Brown

The night can be defined approximately as the time space between the sunset and the sunrise, between the break-in of the darkness and the beginning of the dawn. The clear structures of the day are dissolving until the darkness wraps us.

The sense that mostly characterizes us is our sight. Our eyes close, and other senses awaken (for example, hearing and intuition). In the dark between the day consciousness and sleep, the spirit hikes freer between the worlds and turns inward. The pineal gland starts to produce melatonin, which is necessary for the sleep rhythm.

Many of us are ambivalent about the night. Some are afraid of the night, not only because of supposed ghosts but also because of the rising of their own threatening fantasies, pictures, or memories, or—as the early prehistoric man believed—the dangers in the form of hungry animals. Sleep is also called the little brother of death. Old people, people full of worries, and children sometimes are afraid to fall asleep.

The night is the room of the shadows, uncertainties, nightmares, deceptions, and secret activities ("in the dead of night"), the dark sides of life ("as ugly as sin"), dark and threatening beings ("the night of the long knives"), and somber moods ("as black as night"). The night is simultaneously the room of unconsciousness and its vigors, which have snatched away the power of the light, of consciousness and analytical thought.

In the theogony of the Greek poet Hesiod,[41] Nyx was the goddess of the night, the daughter of chaos, and the mother of heaven and earth. In the Orphic she was the mother of Eros (love). The following creation myth is italicized so that you can directly visualize and internalize it: *In the beginning of all things, there was the black-winged night. Fertilized by the wind, she laid a silver egg in the womb of the darkness. Out of this the sun of the blowing wind rose, a god with golden wings: Eros, the god of love.*[42]

In mythology, the night is said to have various love affairs and children: Aether (the incarnated room) and Hemera (the incarnated day rose from the contact of night and darkness, Nyx and Erebos). Nyx created Hypnos (sleep), Oneiroi (dream), Thanatos (death), and Philotes (affection), and also a series of dreadful beings: ruin, disaster, critics, sorrows, revenge, illusion, age, quarrel, and several others. The night moves over the heaven, wrapped in a dark veil, in a chariot that is drawn by four black horses.

In particular, in the mythology of Nyx, we already find the night connected to the dark desires of this world, but also to creation, lust, and love. Midnight becomes the turning point and the new beginning. At midnight the past is quasi separating from the future. It is the time of the review, the time to face one's shadow, fears, and death. Darkness and being lost are the most prevalent. But where the danger grows, redemption grows too. It is the time of emptiness, as well as fullness. It is the time of the past, as well as the time of the future.

Midnight is the turning point. Midnight is the witching hour insofar as the banned possibilities and beings can stir without the control of the consciousness and may grow. Out of their fullness something new can arise. The midnight is pregnant with the germination of a new day.

In ancient mysteries, midnight is the hour of initiation and spiritual and mental cognition. Apuleius, the Roman author of the Eleusinian mysteries, lets his main actor Lucius shout, "I went until the border between life and death ... at the time of the deepest midnight I saw the sun shine in its brightest light."[43]

This "midnight of the soul" is also described by mystics[44] as an experience of deepest godforsakenness and loneliness. But then comes the moment of repentance, a diving into a new experience of unity. Right now, in this moment of absolute darkness, you shine the light of the world. Yes, you are linking to the light of the world. You are the light of the world.

Breathe out. Breathe out the tensions of your body. Breathe out the darkness of your soul. Look inside. Breathe in the light of midnight. Fulfill your body with deep knowledge, with the feeling (premonition) of eternal, pure light.

Now you can choose. You have infinite possibilities on your path of life at your disposal, no matter what time. Look around!

Imagine your ability to choose even more consciously. I recommend the film and the song with the identically named song, "I Choose Love." It is uniquely pictured and tenderly sung about the freedom to choose and about the freedom to love.

I can see laughter, or I can see tears
I see a choice, love or fear
What do you choose?
I can see peace, or I can see war

I can see sunshine, or I can see a storm
What do you choose?
Now I choose to live with freedom flying
From my heart, where the light keeps shining
I choose to feel the whole world crying
For the strength that we can rise above
I choose Love
I choose Love
I can see sharing, or I can see greed
I can see caring, or poverty
What do you choose?
I can see gardens, or I can see bombs
I can see life, or death
Coming on strong
What do you choose?
Now I choose …
I see us healing, the darkness dying
I see us dawning, as one world united
So what do you choose?
Love or fear
Oh, we choose
Now I choose to live with freedom flying
From my heart, where the light keeps shining
I choose to feel the whole world crying
I choose to feel one voice rising
I choose to feel us all united
In the strength that we can rise above
I choose Love
I choose Love
Oh, I choose Love.[45]

How do you want to decide? Or are you already on your way to being lucky?[46]

Exercise: Choose Love

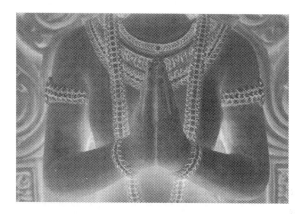

Please close your eyes. Breathe in through your heart and out, and imagine your heart as a lotus that opens and shuts with every breath.

Look above. There your crown is floating on a silver-star stream and sets buoyantly in the middle of your parting. Your vertebrae is balancing it, light and flexible in the posture of your dignity. In the back, two wonderful wings are growing. These might be angel wings, bird wings, or tender butterfly wings. Decide for yourself. Let them flap in the whispering of midnight. Experience how it opens your thorax and your heart for the germs of your future and how they remind your soul in their homeland of freedom.

The treasure of freedom is your fantasy. Fly into the middle of it. Experience freedom and possibilities. Whip out your wand. Revive your inner world, shape it, and change it according to your wishes. Start to conjure. Create your own starry sky. Shape stars that arise in a sparkling explosion of light and those that pass away. Conjure a sparkling sky that welcomes you and a mild shining moon that gives you its light and security. Imagine the earth under you warm and holding. Imagine the midnight wide and mysterious. Conjure the needs of your past into a dark sack, and burn it with fire. Watch how the wind blows the ashes up and away. Recognize how the ashes fertilize the breeding ground for the germs of your future.

Experience the depths of the power inside you to create, develop, and blossom. The magic wand is the mighty tool of your fantasy that creates your life. Sense now the power of freedom to choose and the power of freedom to love.

Dive into the midnight of your soul and the depths of your unconsciousness. Choose love. Breathe in the light, breathe in the love, and breathe in the vision of a healthy, fulfilled life. Flood your body with the wings of luck and harmony until it streams, bubbles, and pulsates. Then all cells will have absorbed the good news of your spirit. Choose love, and then the other exercises will be successful.

Exercise: Shake Out

Look back on this day and the situations that were not kind to love. They were covered with fear, anger, helplessness, hate, or other tensions. Look back on everything that became knotted, on the entanglements with other people or with yourself, or with your own claims, expectations, and impulses.

Now shake off all tensions, all misfortune, and all fear for five minutes. Take some music to it, like "The Foxhunter" If you prefer rock music, try it with "Paint It Black" from the Rolling Stones.

Exercise: Solve Inner Conflicts

After you have liberated and loosened your body from tension, please shut your eyes again. Now look back on the past days. See all the beauty and light moments. Thank them for their wonders with your inner words.

Now turn your inner view to the conflicts of the day. Remember the controversy you had with someone – inward or outward. Zoom out the tensions into a distance. Let your conscious spirit recognize them clearly, compassionately, and without reproach. From this careful distance, look at your own impulses and postures. They can be entangled with your opposite in certain situations or also with yourself.

Recognize which impulses, claims, or postures have led to the conflict. This might be anger, disappointment, expectations, feeling right, feelings of guilt, and more. Recognize yourself without evaluating. See your wounds boldly and without prejudice. Mistakes are our best friends, as they help us to grow.

Write down your realizations. Maybe they are about patterns of habits or attitudes. And when you have clearly recognized your own responsibilities in the conflict, look at them empathically. Experience again your reactions without evaluating them like a film.

And then come nearer again, very near. Slip into and be this other person. Adopt his or her attitude in your thoughts. Perform her or his movements, gestures, and facial expressions. Experience how it is to be this other person. And experience your own behavior with other eyes. Realize injuries, insults, devaluation, or rage.

You know that we all live in our own truth, in our own inner prison in which every action has its own justification. And if you have experienced and recognized the person opposite in his or her individuality, then see yourself. How do you appear in his or her eyes? Sense your effect on your opposite person who you are in this moment.

Then be yourself again. Experience your own truth, which might have changed after this role reversal.

Now imagine how you might have reacted in a different way, how you could have delivered that reaction, satisfied it, or simply left it. Change your behavior now in your imagination and the reaction of your opposite person too. Find a solution for the tension that serves both of you, knowing that everything is connected to everything. Realize that all of your actions have a direct effect on the present moment and on your future. Choose love.

Zoom yourself out of this situation into a distance where you can release it benevolently. Fill it with golden light, and bless it. It has helped you to grow, expand, and deepen. It has helped you to experience and give away your humanity and benevolence. Thank yourself for this performance.

Proceed in this sense with all your entanglements of the day, and exchange them with the prevailing person opposite until all knots and negative tensions are solved.

Then dip the day into golden light, and express your thanks for all experiences of learning. Bless your life.

Sense the silence that grows and develops when the entanglements are detangled, when problems are solved. Experience the relief when challenges become achievements, when faintheartedness becomes greatness, when insecurity becomes strength, and when rage becomes love.

Exercise: Design Your Vision

Let this day pass over to the sheltering darkness. Take your experiences of the setting sun, and see how your own consciousness disappears and gives room to the intuition of your unconscious spirit. Behold how the forms dissolve into a dark emptiness. Look inside, and enjoy the silence of the emptiness, the sheltering darkness, and the womb of the night.

Look inside. Find peace. See how darkness starts to germinate with tomorrow's seed. Face the future now. Tomorrow a new day starts—a new chance to grow, learn, and develop, and a new possibility to change you and the world around you.

What do you want to keep from your attitude toward yourself and life?

What do you want to expand and deepen?

What do you want to change?

Design a vision of yourself that helps you to enjoy a day full of happiness, calmness, and generosity. Create the picture of a fulfilled day. Create a picture of a widely stretched-out, curious, enthusiastic posture of yourself. Embrace tomorrow. Embrace the future. Realize, as Buddha did, that you are today what you have thought yesterday. And you will be tomorrow what you are thinking today.

Conjure a vision of a lucky, healthy, fulfilled life. Imagine it in a detailed and complete way. Behold it with your inner eye. Listen to it with your inner ear. Smell it, taste it, sense it, and internalize it. Make it your own right now. Be the vision of your health, the vision of your happiness.

Write down what you want to change tomorrow, your way to see the world, your behavior, your approach to other people, the possibility to recharge your batteries—whatever it is.

Get up and bring your body into this new direction, which expresses your new vision, so that it internalizes and manifests itself. Form each cell of your body into this new posture. Develop the gestures and facial expressions of confidence and smiling enthusiasm: warm, open, self-assured, anchored in your body as in the stars, and of course with the sparkling crown on your head.

Confirm deep inside: "I am the power to change. I am the creativity of shaping. I am confidence. I am dignity." Dance this new posture for five minutes in the form of a figure eight. Dance the figure eight into the movement of your hips, arms, hands, and feet. Yes, you can even dance the figure eight with your rolling eyes. Play "A Night Like This" by Caro Emerald, "All I Have to Do Is Dream" by The Everly Brothers, "Help Me Make It Through the Night" by Ike and Tina Turner, "Dancing in the Dark" by Bruce Springsteen, "Stairway to Heaven" by Led Zeppelin, or "Night Rain" by Deuter. Find your own song or dance in silence.

Plant the seed of your morning in the womb of the night. Plant the germs of health, happiness, confidence, joy, gratitude, and love.

By midnight, exercise the ability to decide, and to choose, to transform. Every day is different, every day brings something new, and every day is a new chance.

Open the inner and/or outer window, and look into the starry sky. Breathe in the widths of the night. Breathe in the sparkling of the stars. Breathe in the mild glance of the moon. Fulfill yourself with the premonition of the universe and unity. Be the universe, and be united.

MORNING

"You are today what you have thought yesterday.
You are tomorrow what you think today."
—*Buddha*

Eos, the sister of Helios (the sun) and Selene (the moon), was the old Greek goddess of dawn. The Romans called her Aurora. Every morning she announced the new day while appearing drawn by the two horses' "glance" and "lustre" in the east of the horizon. Her brother, Helios, followed her a bit later. With her husband, Astraios, the god of twilight, she had many children (e.g., the four winds and the morning star). Eos was the graceful, beautiful, curly-haired goddess with rose fingers in a saffron-colored dress.

Cat Stevens sings a hymn on the power of the morning:

Mine is the sunlight, mine is the morning
Born of the one light, Eden saw play
Praise with elation, praise every morning
God's recreation of the new day.

The Germans called the goddess of the morning, Fulla. She gave blessings and wealth. Fulla's themes were abundance, protection, cycles, and magic. Fulla was extremely beautiful. Her long, blowing hair mirrored the morning fog. Her most delicate facial color reflected the rose red of the sun. Her jewels were the dewdrops on the meadows. She was the goddess of vegetation and fertility, the goddess of agriculture and the abundance of a fertile earth. She wore a golden ribbon in her hair as a symbol of the ribbon of a grain gift.

She was the goddess of the precious stones, secrets, and mysteries, and she was the custodian of undetected wealth. She gave the power of a young morning and dispelled bad dreams and somber memories. She gave women prosperous lives, delicate skin, the most beautiful jewelry, and a sensual and light life in fullness.

Please close your eyes. Imagine waking up as Fulla every morning: golden, joyous, tender, and full of the mystique of your new day. Imagine waking up as the god of light: shining, powerful, and enlightening. Imagine being beautiful, deeply connected with all the treasures of the new world, and full of excitement for the abundance of your life.

Manuela, a member of my groups, presented me a poem *"Kleine Morgengymnastik"* by Hans Kruppa, which would look like this in English:

> *I get up with the right foot,*
> *open the window of my soul,*
> *bow to everything that lives,*
> *turn my face to the sun,*
> *jump a few times beyond the horizon*
> *and laugh so that I get healthy.*

Manuela developed a physical-psychological gymnastics, lasting only a minute but very effective. She hops out of bed, imagines opening, bows in all four directions, and turns to the light. Then she physically jumps and imagines that it is her inner horizon, and she transcends with every jump. Thus, she imagines widening and expanding her mind. Finally, she laughs and laughs and laughs. Just try it yourself!

In the following longer exercise, you can dive more deeply into the symbolic processes of the morning.

Would you like a fertile life in fullness?
Would you like to shape your day with lush colors?
Would you like to create your happiness yourself?

Exercise: Awaken

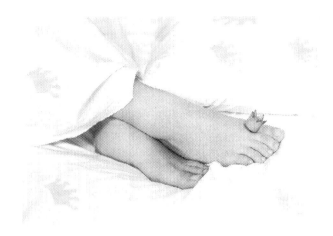

Please close your dear eyes. Breathe in and out through your heart.

Imagine you are lying in your feather-bed, and you are sound asleep. From every cell of your body, fine threads of light spin in the depths of this world and connect you to a waving ocean of light. You are rocked there, and the stars wink at you and watch over your sleep. You dream about peace, happiness, trust, and love. You fantasize wonderful dreams. You see yourself full of confidence, full of cheering encounters and situations, and connected to all of creation. You experience a wonderful world that contains many possibilities and ways for your development. You sleep happily like a little child in the arms of his or her loving mother, the goddess of the night. You are safe, held tight, and relaxed.

After timelessness, your ear is sensing a wonderful melody: the singing of the birds in the morning. Your ear can understand these songs full of happiness and joy over the glowing red sky, over the tender dew, and over the soft wind waving tenderly above the greening grass. The birds tell how the world, with their forms and colors, appears, and how movement slowly awakens. Even the closed calyxes open, trembling.

Your cheek, which is turned to the window, feels the sensual warmth of the morning light, a light tickling.

Wake up, my beauty, my dear, the morning whispers.

Look, the dawn awoke and reaches you now with a tender, golden ray. Not only does the ray tickle your cheek, but you turn your face to it so that it can also tickle your nose, your other cheek, your chin, your soft lips, your eyelids, your ears, and even your hair.

You enjoy this sensual massage, and you push away the blanket slightly so that the ray can kiss your neck, your décolleté, and even your nipple.

Good morning, my beauty. Good morning, my dear, the morning whispers.

You unfold the blanket. The ray spoils your shoulders, arms, hands, and navel. It traces the forms of your hips, snuggles your abdomen and your centers of pleasure, and caresses your thighs lovingly up to your lower legs and your feet.

Give your whole body to the massage of the dawn. Enjoy the tickling and tingling in your whole body. Every cell is saturated with red light, and every cell breathes the clear air of the morning. Every cell awakens, greets you, and attunes to the rhythms of the sun's rays in a subtle way. Every cell breathes in the dawn until your whole body is flooded with new beginning. Even your brain awakens and sparkles with curiosity for this new day. And like the flowers blossom, your heart opens and stretches out toward the red golden splendor and grows to the light. Good morning, dear heavens.

Fill up with vividness, light, sensuality, and overwhelming fullness. You are now prepared for a new experience and the red gold of awakening.

Do you remember what you resolved to do at midnight? Do you remember your new attitude to please this day and to love yourself? Right now is the time to manifest it into your body. Imagine the embodiment of a new beginning. Imagine the embodiment of curiosity, joy, and love for this new day.

Exercise: Get Up

Rise and shine!

Get up enthused in this new posture, which contains your future. Remember that you are dignity, confidence, and courage. You have the infinite creativity to learn, grow, and create.

You are the goddess of dawn, the god of the rising sun.

It is a new day. What a chance!

Get up! Get up into your creative freedom and your confidence. Your crown comes as a golden ray and places itself in the middle of your head. The backbone is already growing toward it and balancing it. The crown gets you in your dignity and in this flexibility, which gives way to every wind of life from one balance to another. Swinging is the basic motion of all beings.

Focus your senses near your backbone. Grow your wings, and open the thorax, widening yourself for this day. Let them flap, and sense the lightness and freedom. Fly like Eos in the sky. Let yourself be guided by gleam and shimmer, knowing that the light will follow you always.

Rise and shine!

Float and fly!

Exercise: Purify

Your first flight leads you into the bathroom. There, you are again getting rid of the old, the past, waste products of your body. Thank your body for the detoxification, for the cleaning. The waste is the excretions of yesterday, which is over forever. Now your body is free for new enjoyment.

Turn on the shower. Sense the tenderness of the warm water flowing over your skin, melting over your face, neck, shoulders, arms, hands, trunk, and down your legs and feet.

Open the skullcap, and let the water float into your brain, taking away the doubts, sorrows, woes, fears, and all the darkness. Let it stream down through your throat into your trunk, cleansing all your inner organs, renewing arms and legs.

Imagine every single cell as cleaned and clear. Visualize your body inward and outward as pure, immaculate, and real, as if it is newly born. Sense yourself as being dewy and crystal clear.

Dry your body now, very tenderly. Put on a protecting coat of lavender scent, rose oil, or chamomile.

Look at yourself in the mirror. Your crown is sparkling in your mirror.

What beauty, grace, purity, and cleanliness! Look how perfect your body is, with movable feet and legs; swinging hips; a well-shaped trunk; movable shoulders, arms, and hands; a swinging head on your shoulders; and an enchanting smile on your lips.

Moreover, look yourself in the eyes! What a sparkling kind of vividness and what a pleasant peace. You are all this.

Exercise: Praise

Look at yourself, and praise yourself with the most beautiful words for three minutes.

Praise your outside and your inside, your past, your present and your future, the vision you can be and want to be—fantasize yourself. Praise yourself for all your talents, for all your potential, and for the possibilities that are opening up.

Hug yourself, caress yourself, and kiss yourself. You are your longest, deepest, and most truthful love of your life. Please start this wonderful love affair now.

Give thanks for your life. Thank your feet for stability, your legs for flexibility, your abdomen for the secrets and pleasures of femininity or masculinity, your trunk for all your inner organs, your shoulders for bearing, your arms and hands for acting, your thyroid for balance, your sensory organs in your head for sensing this world, your heart for love, and your brilliant brain for the ability to recognize and create a fulfilled new day.

Get dressed. Couch yourself with protection, colors, sensuality, and grace. Dress yourself with masculinity or femininity.

Brush your hair until it shines like pure silk. Brush your teeth until they gleam like snow that fell fresh on the earth.

Live your innermost beauty!

Exercise: Celebrate

Open the window, and welcome the morning light.

Breathe in the dawn, and send it to every cell of your body, to every fiber of your being, and into the waters between the cells and the organs. Connect yourself with the power of dawn, the power of a new beginning.

Greet your day. Welcome this new beginning. Hug it, and caress it so it becomes yours. Now your hormones will produce pleasure and enthusiasm for your new day of learning.

How does this new life feel?

How does your body feel?

How does the world feel?

Celebrate your new life.

Today is a new chance, a new luck. It is the morning of your life!

Stride through the room with the new posture, the new dignity, and the new feelings of health and fullness, and behold what happens. Have breakfast with this new posture, meet people with this new attitude, and watch what happens. Yes, even come up to your former enemies with this new attitude, and be aware of what changes. In particular, realize yourself in your fullness, multitude, and infinite creativity.

Hug yourself, hug others, and hug life. Dance your new day enthused in the soil of Mother Earth (if you like, in a figure eight).

Celebrate with Sally Oldfield's "Mirrors."

Dance your new posture for so long that it feels at home within you.

Come, move, dance, dance, dance!

> *Oh we are mirrors in the sun and we brightly shine*
> *We are singing and dancing in perfect time*
> *There is nothing in the world that we can do*
> *To stop the light of love come shining through …*

MIDDAY

"Inflame a sun in you which never expires."
—*Drukpa Rimpoche*

Midday's symbol is golden sunrays. From the beginning of their time, people have likely adored the sun as the source of life. That is why there are a great number of legends, and the sun is playing a particular role in many religions. The motif of a solar barque, in which the sun is floating across the sky, can be found in ancient Egypt in God Ra. In Native American cultures a sun barque floats across the sky. In the Greco-Roman culture, as well as in Nordic mythology, the sun barque was steered by the prevailing sun god.

In ancient Greece, Helios, the sun god, was steering the cart with four splendid horses. His head was surrounded by golden rays. The ancient Romans called the sun god Sol. In ancient Egypt, the sun god was called Re or Ra. The sun is adored there as you see in the image below. Human beings are soaking up the sunlight.

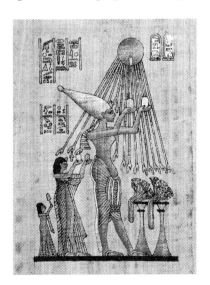

In the north, Brigid, who was surrounded by an aureole, was originally a sun goddess. A story tells that Brigid was born at sunrise and that a tower of flames reached out of her forehead from the earth up to the sky. As a toddler, she slept in a fire ocean. This Brigid energy suppresses the winter and the night.

What we can learn from the sun is that when it comes, it shines. Maybe you can say that of yourself now too!

Similar to midnight, you can organize midday as a time of looking back on the day. Pause for a moment, and enlighten yourself with warmth, light, and golden blessings. Invent your own helpful exercises.

Exercise: Review

Please shut your dear eyes. Breathe out the tensions of the morning. Look back. How did today's morning start? How can you exercise your new attitude? How and when did you fall back into your old patterns? When did you come back home to your inner freedom, and when and how did you get entangled in the expectations of others and your own claims? Have a closer look.

If the last hours were a way, what would it look like? Through which landscapes or light did it lead you? If the last hours were a film, what would it be called? Would it be a tragedy, a comedy, a documentary film, a silent movie, or a soap opera?

If the last hours were a composition of colors, what would the painting look like? Dive deeper into your morning. What were the secret experiences of wisdom? Where was your smile? Where was your dignity? Do you have the crown on your head after all? No? Then look upward, and experience how the sun itself has found your crown again and presents it to you on a sparkling thread. Accept it in a thankful way, and promise anew to take care of it.

It is the shining symbol of your inner dignity, deeply connected to the midday sun. The wings are stuck together. Rise, and let them dry from the warm spring wind. Breathe in freedom anew. Breathe in the pureness, the power of the movement, and its renewal. Remember that you are sixteen, seventeen, or eighteen years old, and life lies ahead of you. It spreads inside you like a vision of fullness, like a colorful meadow. Stretch out your arms, and run into it. Breathe in the scent of the flowers and the blaze of color. Breathe in the richness that is developing before your inner eye.

Exercise: Undo Inner Shackles

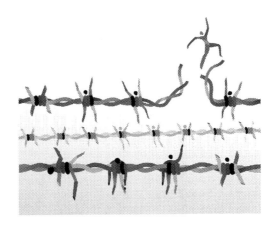

When you have arrived at your inner wealth, look back on the tense situation of this day. Look at your entanglements from the distance of a flowery meadow, and perceive them as in a movie in which you are directing. Then rewind the film to the situation in which the process of entanglement, darkness, and doubt began this morning.

Zoom this moment directly in your eye so that you can see it clearly in slow motion. What happened inside? Realize how you have lost your crown from your morning high. You have exercised enthusiastically, but somehow your posture collapsed, and your body tensed up. You have likely turned your attention too far outward or tried to be nice and well-behaved, or you were driven by the fear of chaos, helplessness, horror, and death.

Develop a picture of these entanglements, fears, sorrows, and doubts. See how they tie up your heart and you can hardly breathe. See how your body becomes a corset, even a prison. Perceive how the chains are restricting you, how the knots are entangling you, and how the inner walls are cementing immovability and fear. Experience again helplessness, horror, and fear.

And then permit all the suppressed fears you had today to show up, spit them out, and unburden yourself of them!

Remember the midnight exercises. Remember that you are free to choose at any time. Do you want the fear? Do you want the tension? Do you want the inner death?

"No, no, and no," I hear you whisper.

"No, no, no," I hear you call.

"No, no, no," I hear you cry.

Then take your sword of light—as if by magic it still lies in your hands—raise it to the sun, and charge it with fire, life, and clarity. With the power of your will, cut up the chains, and unravel the entanglements. Cut through your inner shackles, and undo and relieve the knots.

Turn the sword into a magic wand, and break the iron rings. Imagine the knots are opening or that you find the key that opens the doors of your prison. With the creativity of your spirit, the clearness of your mind, and the warmth of your loving heart, free yourself!

Understand yourself as the reason for distress, fighting, cramping, and other problems. Your own inner attitude has created it. The good news is a new attitude and direction can release them and has already loosened them.

Experience the power that lies in the infinite freedom of your will and your mind. Experience the power of creativity. Play with your possibilities to remove the deadlocks. Compare your various attitudes toward life. Life can be a permanent fight, a game, a school, a book, or a dance. Decide for yourself. Which attitude makes life successful?

Remove the tension of the last hours with the power of your creative imagination, and stand up anew in your dignity, inner strength, and abundance!

Exercise: Enlighten Yourself

Look up to the sun. Do you see how it sparkles in the sky? It donates life, warmth, and energy to all of us. Let it caress you with its rays. Breathe in the light through your heart, and fulfill it with shine.

With every breath, soak up light and breathe out darkness. Breathe in warmth, and breathe out stiffness. Breathe in energy, and breathe out faintness. Fulfill yourself with the sparkling of the sky, and send it into your feet. Become aware that your feet will forward it in roots of light that grow deep into the depths of the earth and keep you safe in this earthly homeland. Feel yourself firm and anchored in a loving way.

Send the light into the soles of your feet, and massage them from the heels to the toes and back to the heels. Create sensual experiences of closeness, and sense how the streaming in the heels connects with the pulsating of the earth and anchors you in a sensory way.

Continue to breathe in the sunlight and pour it over your feet. Enlighten every single toe, and sense every cell. Enlighten the ankles, and see how the light is swinging. Breathe in the light in your lower legs. Caress the skin, and then go into it. Bring the light into every muscle fiber, every bone, and every single cell. Continue to breathe, and send the energy of light into your knees. Imagine your knees flooded with light, which swings in soft waves. Breathe in movability. Send the light into your thighs. Massage the fine skin and every fiber inside you. Imagine your legs as bright, clear, and pulsating.

Imagine that you continue to go up with your loving attention. Let your centers of delight dance in the ray of sunshine—soft, wild, tender, and free.

Continue to breathe in the sunlight. Guide it upward into your coccyx and vertebrae up the spinal column. Massage every vertebra with light, love, and warmth. Let your spinal column become a swinging tube in the cornfield through which the midday sun floods—stable by movability.

Soak up the sunlight into your inner organs. Enlighten your stomach, intestines, liver, gallbladder, pancreas, spleen, kidney, and bladder until they stream and sparkle with warmth and feel-good feelings.

Let the light flood wide and free through your lungs. Let the light purify every pore, and open it for the breath of life! Breathe the light into your thyroid, and imagine it as a tender butterfly. Experience how it develops into the sun's rays and swings very fine in the melody of balance. Discover that its vibrations take your whole body into a pleasant harmony.

Soak up the light in your head. Let the sun's rays caress your chin, your cheeks, and your forehead. Let the sun's rays purify your nose and clean and caress your ears. Let the sun's rays kiss the tender skin of your lips. Let yourself be aroused sensually for this day.

Dispense the light over your parting chakra inside your brain. Bathe every cell there in light, purity, and warmth. Imagine your brain is enlightened, sparkling, and swinging free in the streams of love. Realize how it connects with your heart. Both are embracing intimately.

Change your body field into a choppy ocean of lights, every organ an octave of love, the whole body a symphony of an enlightened life. Please confirm inside you: "I am clarity. I am shining. I am warmth. I am the flame of life. I am the light."

Now save these experiences in every cell, in every fiber of your being, in the creative networks of your brain, and in the wide open love of your heart. Look at the afternoon as it dances in the swings of light, streams in the waves of luck, and pulsates in the beats of its wings of your open heart.

Dance the enlightenment into the world, into your life, and into your future. Dance in the here and now. For example, listen to "Paradise Is Here" by Tina Turner:

'Cause paradise is here
it's time to stop your crying
the future is this moment
and not some place out there'

Swing to "Be" by Neil Diamond. Should you prefer tones that are quiet, listen to Deuter's "SunSpirit" or "Sunlight Dancing," or simply enjoy pure sunlight.

EVENING

"Learn to let go. This is the key to luck."
                    —*Buddha.*

Astraios is the god of the twilight. He fathered his four children, the winds and the morning star, also known as the evening star, with Eos, the dawn. Ausrine, who is probably etymologically related to Aurora, the Roman morning goddess who presents in Baltic mythology as the goddess of love and dawn, corresponds to the goddess Venus. She is also adored as the epitome of beauty, youth, and health, as she blossoms in the beautiful light of dawn and dusk. She announces the new day and the beginning of the silence of the night. She appears to be eternal, young, and healthy—in the morning, as well as in the evening. Just the same as you!

Breathing in this light with a pure heart, we are allowed to forgive, transform, and reconcile.

Exercise: Forgive

Forgiveness is always a decision. It does not come from a religious superego or a moral postulate but from the middle of your heart in its desire for inner freedom. Even if it is difficult for you in the present moment and appears to be strange, imagine how you forgive. Regularly exercise the liberating feelings of grace, and greatness will soon follow. Trust the process.

Please shut your eyes. Breathe out the tensions of the afternoon. Pause.

Recognize the unpleasant situations and the moments of tension and fear. Look back on the moments of disappointment, injury, and insult. Remember the people you hold responsible for the sufferings of this day, including yourself.

Let all feelings that were suppressed until now arise. Give them room, and let them expand until they run out. Let go of the physical tensions. Understand both as a fundamental sign of humanity, which has mastered surviving with fear of failure. Today's activating situation that has produced it is over now, just as the enigmatic primal experience of the fears.

Say good-bye to them.

You are free forever to welcome a new presence.

Shake out these unpleasant feelings—out of the feet, out of the legs, out of the lower abdomen, out of the trunk, out of the shoulders, out of the arms and hands, out of the head, out of the centers of your memory, and out of the fear centers of your brain. Free yourself from tensions, fear, and everything that is unpleasant. Dance wild to "Born to Be Wild" by Steppenwolf or "Scream and Shout" by Britney Spears and will.i.am.

Even after having liberated yourself emotionally from resentment, hate, fear, injury, and insult, you can prepare yourself for forgiveness. Guess the space of freedom inside you—the freedom to choose fear or love.

Choose love.

Now invite these persons who have hurt you today on your inner stage. Sense them, and embody your courage and freedom. Imagine forgiveness. Rise into your divinity, greatness, and generosity. The crown sparkles on your head, the wings swing in the wind of freedom, and the smile of grace shines to your ears. Imagine the fullness of your being, and experience yourself connected to the wisdoms of life.

Approach these people. Look into their eyes directly from the center of your soul. Recognize that your counterpart is a human being, just as you are, with mistakes, weaknesses, and very special ways of learning.

Speak the words: "For my own sake, for the peace of my soul, for the peace of the day, and for the peace of the night, I forgive you. I forgive you for your insults, your emotional cruelties, your ignorance, your arrogance, your devaluation, and your carelessness. I forgive you out of my wide heart now and forever. I recognize in you my mirror image for my own inconsistencies, my own humanness, my own twists and turns, and my own desires and fears. For the sake of my night's harmony, I forgive you. For the peace of my sleep, I forgive you. For here and now I forgive you." Repeat at your own tempo the liberating mantra: "I forgive you, I forgive you, I forgive you." Experience liberation, lightness, and thankfulness for the love in your heart.

Looking even deeper, recognize both of your souls in a waving field of energy and ocean of light. Realize how each of your movements takes the other one with you. You do not exist separately from each other. Sense the closeness of the whole creation and how your own forgiveness gets not only you but also the whole cosmos into a harmonic oscillation.

In this way, deal with all human beings over whom you have thrown reproach, fear, or shadows. Excuse and forgive them.

Now you can look at yourself in the course of the day. Approach yourself and say, "My love, I forgive you for of all your rudeness, carelessness, learned automatisms. I forgive you for your mistakes and privations. Here and now I recognize the inherent possibilities to learn, grow, and develop. I forgive you, and I thank you." And then embrace yourself, comfort yourself, encourage yourself, and love yourself.

Look back on this day. Experience its new moments of luck, joy, and fulfillment, and save them in your body. Repeat inside, "What a wonderful day. Thank you!"

With some songs of forgiveness and thankfulness, you can dance this new freedom in your body and in the soil of Mother Earth. Sing to yourself and to others, "I love you just the way you are." Dance to "Just the Way You Are" by Billy Joel.

I take you just the way you are.
I said I love you.
And that's forever.

Exercise: Let Go

Please shut your dear eyes. Breathe in and out through your heart. Experience your body as pulsating and swinging, pleasant and warm. Prepare your farewell of the day. Imagine you are pulling off the old roles and automatisms with your clothes, until you are only the essence of your being—light, lucid, and clear. Take a shower, and experience how the water cleans every pore, flows inside, and streams and purifies every cell, organ, and even interspace. Two-thirds of your body consists of water. Visualize yourself as a crystal-clear sea that is waving in the vibration of the dust, breathing in the last sunrays, as well as the darkness. Experience how this sea reflects the rising of the moon and the birth of the stars— mysteriously, wide, and full of magic. All this is what you are!

Let this sea inside you dance and wave to "So Much Magnificence" by Deva Premal and Miten.

NIGHT

*"Sleep is the umbilical cord the individual
is connected to the universe."*
—*Friedrich Hebbel*

In Greek mythology, Hypnos is the god of sleep. His Roman counterpart is Somnus. Hypnos is the son of Nyx (night) and Erebus (darkness). He is the brother of Thanatos (death), and both are living in the underworld. His children are the deities of the dream: Morpheus (shape), Phobetor (horror), and Phantasos (fantasy). He flies with his mother over the night sky.

Hypnos is often presented as a sleeping youth garlanded with opium poppies or as a graceful young man with butterfly wings over his temples. According to Greek mythology, Hypnos has the power to move all gods and goddesses and all human beings and animals into a deep sleep.

In our imagination, we are working with a kind of auto-Hypnos-is. We are turning into a vibration and mood, similar to a trance or sleep.

Sleep is a state of external silence; the pulse, breathing rate, and blood pressure reduce, and the brain activity changes. Shutting the eyes excludes many sensory inputs, and the attention focuses inside. In the dream phases, the pulse, breath, and heartbeat can be stimulated and increased again, depending on what is happening in the dreams.

The basis for the development of silence and activity cycles was probably given to us by the rotation of the earth, with its rhythm of day and night, which is unchangeable for all organisms. Depending on the time of day, the blossoms of plants are opening and closing. Even single-celled organisms, such as a flagellum *Lingulodinium polyedrum*, orient their activities to the position of the sun. The observations of less developed organisms suggest that adapting to light and temperature has already happened early in the evolution for regulating metabolic activities.

It is supposed that the necessity to sleep has developed simultaneously with the development of neuronal networks, which were getting more and more complex. Accordingly, there is a direct relation between the demand of sleep and the productivity of the brain, particularly concerning the processing and saving of information. So we can compare the brain with a computer that has achieved its maximum working capacity even when all external sensory impressions and its processing are switched off. Only in the sleep phase can the "computer" brain serve with its entire computing power.

Our inner clock is essentially responsible for a regular circadian rhythm. For healthy people it consequently is in accordance with the change of day and night, of light and dark. This inner clock is decisively responsible for the hormone balance of the body; therefore, it regulates our need for sleep.

Three groups of nerve cells essentially participate in starting sleep. These groups of nerve cells belong to the area of brainstem known as the *Formatio reticularis*, and two further interbrain areas called the thalamus and the hypothalamus. The *Formatio reticularis* is known for functioning as a signal head for alertness. It practices its attention or waking function via chemical messengers with which it stimulates the thalamus as the "gate to consciousness."

It is true that in Greek, *thalamus* means "bedchamber." However, it is more of an awaking room that specializes in the passing on of sensory stimuli to the great brain. Above the so-called bedroom lives another neural system, the hypothalamus, which steers important vegetative closed-loop control circuits and which seems to be responsible for the circadian rhythm.

The hypothalamus is connected to the visual pathway. In darkness it decisively influences the release of melatonin from the pineal gland. Melatonin is stopped by light so that it increasingly can be released in the evening hours, and it contributes to start sleep. Consequently, the brain learns from the hypothalamus that it is time to sleep as it gets dark. In the course of the night, melatonin is increasingly released.

During healthy sleep, the nerve cell organizations start to synchronize. This means that they fire their action potentials in a joint rhythm. By diverting electrical streams via an electroencephalogram (EEG), various rhythms can be measured and made visible. According to the depth of the sleep and the characteristic patterns that are connected to it, sleep can be divided into various stadia. Depending on the frequency and height of these inner brain waves, the following stadia and the corresponding waves can be distinguished, whereby the concrete classification of the sleep stadia is arbitrary indeed:

1. Attention: beta waves (14 to 30 Hz)
2. Relaxing with closed eyes: alpha waves (8 to 13 Hz)
3. Light sleep just before falling asleep: brain turning from alpha waves to theta waves (4 to 7 Hz). The muscle tension is getting reduced, and the conscious sensing of the surroundings is slowly disappearing.
4. Deep sleep: delta waves (0.1 to 4 Hz, slow waves with a high amplitude) now coming to the fore (20 to 50 percent of the brain waves that were measured), and muscle tension decreasing more and more
5. REM sleep (rapid eye movement, also called dream sleep): distinguished in many ways from other sleep phases. The

EEG is similar to sleep stadium 1 (predominantly theta waves). However, in regular intervals there are quick movements of the eyeball with a frequency of 1 to 4 Hz, which are lacking direction. Dream reports while waking from sleep in this phase are significantly more vivid, visual, and emotional than waking from sleep in other phases. During REM sleep, the skeleton muscles, except the eye muscular system, are relaxed in a maximum way. However, many vegetative functions are activated. Even adrenaline can be released.

During sleep the individual body systems synchronize again to a joint rhythm of the process. Most likely after sufficient and relaxing sleep, all organs and other functions of the body begin to correspond to their imposed inner program, but they experience different speeds and irregularities throughout the day.

The best bridge between the banks of despair and the banks of new hope is a night well slept through. At night we sleep with our eyes shut.

We can even choose a good night sleep.

In every moment we choose and, thus, create our alleged reality. You might remember the song of midnight, "I Choose Love." If not, then turn back and fix it in your memory. Internalize every word until you know with closed eyes that the big might of life lies inside you. You can always choose. Choose love!

What a risk to sacrifice your main sense and to entrust to the insecure secrets of every night. Yes, we give up control. Our brain is waving in soft unconsciousness. Our brain waves in a lullaby. Imagine yourself an the exercise to this sentence. Write it down right now, choose corresponding music, and choose the peace of your breath that is getting more and more silent. Breathe in the width of the starry sky, and breathe in the sparkling of the night!

Exercise: Thank

Let this day recall the past. Thank each of your breaths, your heartbeat, your inner organs, and every cell. Thank the dawn, the luminousness of midday, the dusk of the evening, and the secret of the night. Give thanks for the encounters, challenges, and solutions. Thank the vividness of your life. Dapple golden light over all beings and all interspaces. Experience them as connected and flooded by luck.

Experience: Trust

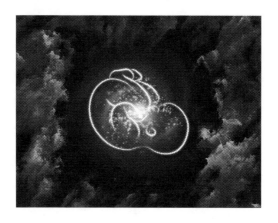

When we were babies, we slept eighteen hours daily, probably without fear. We probably also slept in the womb. Our eyes were closed.

Imagine you are very small and you sway in the warm womb of fertility. You rock in security. You are nourished, provided for, and held in a breathing cave of love. Breathe in the darkness as a holding energy. Breathe in the night as the secret of life. Experience how you can let go, trust, and slumber sweetly. Experience the basic trust in each cell of your body.

The night serves the processing of the day, the regeneration, and the connection to the widths of this world, which I call the ocean of creation. Sense beyond your consciousness how you are connected widely in this world and how you are a wave in the ocean of creation. Enjoy the night.

Exercise: Come into Balance

In the night the parasympathetic system takes the lead and streams through your body with the sensations of silence, harmony, and peace. The *nervus vagus*, arising from the prolonged spinal cord, calms your breath and your inner organs.

Please go with your loving attention to your prolonged upper peak to your cervical spine. Caress it with imaginary hands, and kiss it with soft lips. Caress it until streaming and pulsating sensations develop there.
From there on, a stream is flooding, which medicine calls nervus

vagus. Bless it with love and peace, fulfill it with warm light, and flood it with the starry sky. Massage and caress its tangled roots, anchor it, and secure it in your brain.

Follow its inner course. Experience how it flows to your thyroid, how it embraces it tenderly, and how it lends it the vibrations of the night. Look at how the thyroid swings in the waves of the moonlight, calm and in harmony. Continue to follow the river, and experience how it streams through your lungs and waves in lullabies, how it touches your heart and fulfills it deeply with thankfulness, how it continues to stream into your stomach and intestines and into the inner organs, how it embraces it with peace and silence, and how the whole trunk breathes like a sea in the starry sky. Experience the essence of deep peace.

Exercise: Open

Go to the window, open it, and breathe in the starry sky. Send this infinite width into your legs and feet. Fulfill your femininity and masculinity with the starry sky. Fulfill all your inner organs with starlight and moonlight. Send the sparkling light of the stars into your shoulders, arms, and legs. Let the starlight flow through your thyroid, face, ears, mouth, nose, and eyes. Let the stars play with your hair. Open your cranium, and let the night sky flood into it. Wrap it in a covering darkness, peace, romance, and softness. Imagine that your whole body is penetrated by the secrets of the night, and every cell in the body is a bright, sparkling star.

Imagine how the night rocks every cell, calms them, caresses them, and sings a lullaby. All cells are resting, full of trust in the power of the night, to solve, reconcile, relax, and arrange anew. All cells are slumbering in the same rhythm, in a unity that echoes in your body, deeply reassuring. Sleep soft and blessed full of trust.

Sense how the angels place somewhere to your right and to your left, just as the old song promises.

When at night I go to sleep,
Fourteen angels watch do keep,
Two my head are guarding,
Two my feet are guiding;
Two upon my right hand,
Two upon my left hand.
Two who warmly cover
Two who o'er me hover,
Two to whom 'tis given
To guide my steps to heaven.
Sleeping softly, then it seems
Heaven enters in my dreams;
Angels hover round me,
Whisp'ring they have found me;
Two are sweetly singing,
Two are garlands bringing,
Strewing me with roses
As my soul reposes.
God will not forsake me
When dawn at last will wake me.[47]

While you are slumbering, soft and blessed, a dream is waving out of the middle of yourself.

Exercise: Bless

Please shut your eyes. Breathe in and out through your heart. Imagine a lotus blossom that is opening and shutting with every breath. All negativity, doubts, worries, and fears are running up in pearls. The lotus is always pure and opens to the light.

Sense your crown on your cranium as a symbol of your dignity, the great wings as a sign of your widths and freedom, and the smiling wisdom that plays about your lips as an expression of your love of life.

Look at the rhythms of becoming and passing away.

Imagine the course of the sun, the dawn, the warm rays of the south, and the dusk. Experience the course of the moon and the stars.

Take care of the greater rhythms. Breathe in the spring, and sense how it turns into summer. Then it becomes chillier. The fog of autumn covers the country until the snow falls and wraps everything in a white cotton wool—and then again in the first germination of the green. Experience how a flower germinates, develops, blossoms, and then drops its blossoms and leaves and withdraws into the earth.

Now focus your loving attention inside. Follow the rhythm of your breath, of your heart, and of your beat of an eyelash. Perceive your metabolism and the circulation of your blood. All these rhythms serve the stabilization and balance of your life. When the rhythms stand idle (i.e., when change does not take place), material life expires. Life and change are one.

Visualize an opening at your cranium through which you are slipping. Sense how the field of your body expands in manifold waves. See how it can form into a golden ladder, and enter the first step full of amazement. It bears you, and courageously you climb up the ladder. See your room from some distance. Continue to climb. See your place of residence below you, then your country, and then your continent, with all its mountains, valleys, rivers, seas, meadows, pastures, animals and plants. Continue to take steps on the golden ladder until you leave behind the earth, past the moon, the planets, and the sun, and go on through the Milky Way, the galaxies, and the stardust. See stars explode, implode, come into being, and pass by. Continue to climb on the golden ladder through the whole world. Climb higher and higher, until you leave this universe of room and time. Take steps, pause, and look back. The universe has been reduced to the size of a football, then to the size of an orange, then to a walnut, and last but not least to a spark that becomes extinct.

Continue to rise higher and higher. Become lighter and freer on your way into light. Come to the colors of the rainbow, which breaks the light. Climb through the red light, then the orange light, the yellow light, the green light, the light-blue light, the dark-blue light, and last but not least the violet light. You are finally there. Enter the bright, glorious light.

Bathe in light. Light wraps, penetrates, and fulfills you. Dissolve into this pure, clear light. You are the light, and the light is you. You are pure light. Enjoy fulfillment!

After timelessness you start to form a new vision out of light, like the gods and goddesses, which shape the human beings out of clay. Lay all your creativity, love, and grandeur in this work of art that you are yourself. Look at yourself in your new beauty, and enter this composition of light. You are your vision. You are healthy, happy, and perfect. Enjoy your new being to the fullest.

After further eternities you open the gates back into your earthly life. From the uppermost place sprinkle many golden light blessings below, and let them stream on your sleeping being and enlighten every cell. Bless your past, your present, and your future. Bless all human beings and their life on earth.

Descend step by step through the violet, blue, green, yellow, orange, and red lights, and enter this universe of room and time. Climb through the canopy of stars, our solar system, until you see your earth home and the gravity that is now starting to tighten you and make your location visible.

See yourself lying in a relaxed way. In a cascade of sparkling light rush into a new, healthy, happy body. Sense how all cells unite to cheer in your whole being. Congratulations to your rejuvenation! Sense in each of your cells, in your whole being, that when you awake, the most beautiful day of your life begins!

TIME TO SAY FAREWELL

*"Look and you will find; what is not looked
after will remain undiscovered."*

—*Sophocles*

And now, after all the many inspirations, pictures, and stories, please take your time and develop your own rituals for day and night.

Imagine you are always connected to your innermost source. It is called creativity. Let it bubble freely. There is no right or wrong. Your body decides the effectiveness of the experiences. So take care with every exercise. Know that your body has accepted the exercise and implemented it. Through it new networks are built in the brain, and a new posture is born. You can enrich, fulfill, and heal your life.

Execute the exercises you have composed for a month with enthused will. Then pause and sense what happens.

What has changed?

What is still blocking you?

What will you let go of next month?

Check your rituals, change them, and adjust them! Congratulate yourself for each of your successes, and thank yourself for every step into your own completeness.

Look deeply into the mystique of time, and know that right now is always the time to start something new and to trust the magic of life.[48]

One More Time

"And time dissolves in the depths of our love."

I want to tell you one last story.

A wise man asked his pupils, "Can you tell me how you can determine the hour when the night ends and the day begins?"

Somebody said, "Maybe when you can distinguish a dog from a sheep from a distance?"

"No," answered the master.

"When you can distinguish a date from a fig tree?" asked a disciple.

They gave several answers, and the master denied them all. Finally, he said, "Well, I will reveal it to you. The day starts when you can look into the face of a human being, and you can see your brother or your sister in it. Until then night is still there with us."[49]

Look, the sun is rising. It is becoming morning.

BIBLIOGRAPHY

Braden, Gregg. *Im Einklang mit der göttlichen Matrix.* Auflage: Koha, Burgrain, 2009. *The Devine Matrix*

Dispenza, Joe. *Ein neues Ich – Wie Sie Ihre gewohnte Persönlichkeit in vier Wochen wandeln können.* Koha, Burgrain, 2012. *Breaking the Habit of Being Yourself*

Gibran, Khalil. *Sämtliche Werke.* Patmos, Düsseldorf, 2003. *The Complete Works*

Grün, Anselm. *50 Rituale für das Leben.* Spektrum, Freiburg: Herder, 2011

Jung, Carl Gustav. Das symbolische Leben. Walter, Olten, 1939. *The Symbolic Life*

Jung, Carl Gustav. Der Mensch und seine Symbole. Walter, Olten, 1988. *Man and His Symbols*

Jung, Carl Gustav. Synchronizität, Akausalität und Okkultismus. dtv, München, 1990. *Synchronicity: An Acausal Connecting Principle*

Jung, Carl Gustav. *Über die Entwicklung der Persönlichkeit*, Band 17, Walter, Olten, 1988. *The Development of Personality*

Jung, Carl Gustav. *Die Dynamik des Unbewussten. The Structure and Dynamic of the Psyche*

Kleeberg, Alexandra. *Das Buch der Selbstheilung – Mit Imaginationen die inneren Potentiale stärken und entfalten.* Via Nova, Petersberg, 2013.

Müller, Anette und Lutz.Wörterbuch der Analytischen Psychologie. Patmos, Düsseldorf, 2003.

Penrose, Roger. Zyklen der Zeit. Spektrum, Heidelberg, 2011. *Cycles of Time*

Sheldrake, Rupert. Das schöpferische Universum. Füllstein, Berlin, 2009. *A New Science of Life*

Tolle, Eckhart. Jetzt! Auflage: Kamphausen, Bielefeld, 2010. *The Power of Now*

Weber, Renée. Wissenschaftler und Weise. Rowohlt, Reinbek 1992. *Dialogues with Scientists and Sages*

ENDNOTES

1. An Irish blessing
2. Old wisdom, probably from Sanskrit or the Talmud.
3. Reference to a saying of the Indian theologian Anthony de Mello.
4. The former monk Chögyam Trungpa speaks about panorama consciousness, referring to the spirit being as wide as the firmament.
5. C.G. Jung, *Das Symbolische Leben* (1939). *The Symbolic Life*
6. C.G. Jung, *Der Mensch und seine Symbole* (Aufl. Olten: Walter, 1988), S. 95. *Man and His Symbols*
7. "Try" from the singer Pink.
8. Ecclesiastes 3 King James Version (KJV)
9. I choose these two different spellings to make them easier to distinguish
10. Orphism is a religious tendency from the sixth and seventh centuries BC, which refers to Orpheus. See also https://en.wikipedia.org/wiki/Orphism.
11. http://science-of-involution.org/de/Artikel/Vedische Kosmogonie.html. (2013).
12. Roger Penrose: *Cycles of Time*.
13. Quelle: http://www.heartmath.org/research/science-of-the-heart/entrainment coherence-autonomic-balance.html.
14. Byrds, Turn! Turn! Turn! http://www.radioberlin.de/musik/popgeschichten/dokumente/byrds.html
15. You can even buy this slogan on a T-shirt.
16. Carl Gustav Jung distinguishes three kinds of synchronicity: 1. The coincidence of a psychological circumstance of an observer with the simultaneous objective event happening outside, which corresponds to a psychological situation or contents 2. As above, the event outside cannot be verified immediately but only afterward. 3. As above, only the event outside is in the future, and, therefore, it can be verified only at a later point of time.
17. Carl Gustav Jung, *Collected Works*, 8, Walter, Olten, 1987, §972.
18. Boethius, *De Trinitate* 4, 70.
19. David Bohm in Renée Weber (Ed.) in: Wissenschaftler und Weise, 1992. *Dialogues with Scientists and Sages*
20. Khalil Gibran: Sämtliche Werke, Düsseldorf: Patmos, 2003, S. 855. *Collected Works*

21 In Gregg Braden, Im Einklang mit der göttlichen Matrix, p.107. *The Devine Matrix*

22 http://de.wikipedia.org/wiki/Relativit%C3%A4tstheorie#Relativit.C3.A4t von Raum und Zeit.

23 www.wasistzeit.de.

24 David Bohm in Renée Weber, *Dialogues with Scientists and Sages*, 1986.

25 Khalil Gibran, *The* Prophet, Horizon, 1923.

26 C.G. Jung GW: Synchronizität, Akausalität und Okkultismus, München: Dtv, 1990, S. 63. *Synchronicity: An Acausal Connecting Principle*

27 e.g.. Krishnamurti, *Collected Works.*

28 e.g.. Meister Eckhart, Mystische Schriften. *Mystic Writings*

29 This saying was assigned to various cultures. I could not clarify its origin.

30 Eckhart Tolle, Jetzt! S.50. *The Power of Now*

31 Eckhart Tolle, *Jetzt!* S.52. The Power of Now

32 Rumi, Dschalal ad-Din Muhammad Rumi, Persian mystic, 1207–1273.

33 Thich Nhat Hanh.

34 Chamelie Ardagh.

35 Childre, Doc/Martin,Howard: Die Herzintelligenzmethode, VAK, Kirchzarten, 2000, Seite 25, 29. *Heartmath*

36 http://www.wissen.de/wortherkunft/i-routine.

37 Carl Gustav Jung, Über die Entwicklung der Persönlichkeit, Band 17, Walter, Olten, 1988, § 305, § 308, § 317. *The Development of Personality*

38 http://www.welt.de/gesundheit/psychologie/article106140349/Warum-eshilft-wenn-die-Milch-immer-rechts-steht.html.

39 Joe Dispenza, Ein neues Ich: Wie Sie Ihre gewohnte Persönlichkeit in vier Wochen wandeln können, Koha, Burgrain, 2012. *Breaking the Habit of Being Yourself*

40 Idem.

41 About 700 BC.

42 http://www.schlangengesang.de/archiv/37.pdf.

43 Ugo Bianchi: The Greek Mysteries. Brill, Leiden 1976, ISBN 90-04-04486-8 (Iconography of religions 17, 3, ISSN 0169-9822).zitiert nach http://de.wikipedia.org/wiki/Mysterien von Eleusis.

44 Johannes vom Kreuz, Theresa von Avila etc.

45 With friendly approval and millionfold encouragement of Shawn Gallaway. Cordial thanks!

46 Picture of a participant of my group. Thank you very much!

47 Engelbert Humperdinck (1854–1921), from the opera *Hänsel und Gretel, Evening Prayer of Fourteen Angels*

48 Referring to Meister Eckhart.

49 Chassidic story http://www.zeitblueten.com/news/wann-endet-die`-nacht-und-beginnt-der-tag/.

50 Flickr, Alice Popcorn - Guardian of Time

51 Flickr, Jinterwas - Golden times - you & me - fading into memory

About the Author

Dr. Alexandra Kleeberg is a clinical psychologist, Jungian psychoanalyst, psychodrama- and behavioral therapist. She studied shamanism for 20 years. Alexandra is the author of six books on self-healing - published in English *Self-Healing: Nine Steps Into the Wealth of Health,* and two children's books *You Are Extraordinary and You Are Heartful.* She is a trainer and expert of self-healing in groups in Germany and Austria.

For the past four decades, Alexandra explored the techniques and benefits of self-healing from ancient cultures and modern research around the world. Her system "Self-Healing by Embody-Mental Imagination" (SHEMI) empowers people to tap into their very own power of self-healing.

Alexandra combines medicine and psychology, ancient wisdom and new research, practical experiences and enthusiastic visions to teach clients and therapists the power to self-heal. The result was her clients got inspired, empowered and felt deeply supported. Not only that Alexandra felt more energy, joy and creativity, Alexandra discovered it is more powerful for people to self-heal. They have more fun, are more creative, find their dignity and emotional freedom – as well as the psychotherapists.

From the Wisdom of Your Body
From the Freedom of Your Mind
From the Love of Your Heart
Arises a Deep Might
The Power to Heal Yourself

(Alexandra Kleeberg)

Follow Me

Wouldn't it be awesome if the power of imagination, which distinguishes us from any other living being, and which is always with us, would already be taught in kindergarten, school, business and families? Imagine how people dissolve their fears, understand the miracles of the functioning of their body, know how to heal most diseases, discover their full potential, develop self-esteem and learn how to inspirit hearty relations with others.

To spread this vision into the world I offer knowledge, wisdom and experiences concerning self-healing on different platforms:

On **Facebook Evision Publishing,** you find blogs and our Tuesday 8pm UCT Evision Live broadcast on self-healing, potential development and the power of imagination.

On my **YouTube Channel Alexandra Kleeberg,** you find many videos, interviews and speeches to dive deeper into the power of self-healing.

As a daily reminder, I offer the newsletter **HeartLight** – 1001 imaginations and exercises to widen and deepen your imagination.

You can subscribe on http://.evisionpublishing.com. Here are three examples of the **HeartLight** newsletter:

You can also subscribe **30 Days of Gratitude** and get a gratitude exercise every day for 30 days. By purchasing this book you will get free access to the **Discover Shemi** membership site. Just go to and register at http://evisionpublishing.com. To get a free guided imagination of one of the imaginations in this book, please send an email to order@evisionpublishing.com with the subject line HEDBONUS MP3. You can become a member in my facebook group **Self-Healing and Potential development** under https://www.facebook.com/groups/180018442642698/.

The book *Self- Healing: Nine Steps into the Wealth of Health* provides a systematic guide on how you can discover, awaken and strengthen your healing powers in nine simple steps. The easy to follow nine steps to healing include exercises, imaginations, case studies and success stories. While *Healing Every Day* enables you to create self-healing rituals in your everyday life, the *Nine Steps Into the Wealth of Health* are a structured approach to learning and teaching Self-healing. Both books complete each other. You can order the book and 20 MP3s that come with it via https://evisionpublishing. com/shop-english/

Know Thyself

Do you feel exhausted, discouraged, burnt-out, or often sick? You have the power to change that! You can choose a healthy, fulfilled and happy life. This book provides a systematic guide on how to discover, awaken and strengthen your self-healing powers in 9 steps. This essentially happens through the power of your embody-mental imagination, which deeply affects your body, your consciousness, your social relationships, and ultimately, all of life. Twenty comprehensible exercises will help you on your way to healing. Be prepared to profoundly experience yourself and your life differently.

About the Author

Dr. Alexandra Kleeberg, works as a Jungian psychoanalyst, Psychodrama therapist, and behavioral therapist in her own practice in Lindau, Germany. She applies modern research to ancient healing wisdom

From her over 35 years of psychotherapeutical work and group teachings, she has developed a systematic approach to invigorate self-healing powers. She developed SHEMI – self-healing by embody-mental imagination - which integrates different approaches, exercises and imaginations into a profound meta system that serves the development of self-healing worldwide. She trains practitioners from medical, psychological, social, wellness and educational backgrounds in an online as well as a live certification program.

She is well-known through lectures, media appearances and her books *The Book of Self-Healing, Healing Every Day*, the *You Are Extraordinary, You Are Heartful* children's series, and as co-author of the bestseller, *The Prosperity Factor* with Dr. Joe Vitale.

Alexandra Kleeberg

Self-Healing

Nine Steps Into the Wealth of Health

Embodi-mental exercises and imaginations for a healthy happy life

My doctor colleague Michael Schlaadt and I founded **Network Self-Healing.** Our goal is to get 1001 healing stories in 1001 days. We publish them on our website, so that everybody can have access to it.

I also offer online courses and trainings for medical, psychological, wellness, social, health, coaching professionals. You can get much more information and inspiration on the website http://evisionpublishing.com. There you get access to the other books I wrote, my audios and videos.

My vision is to bring SHEMI (self-healing by embody-mental imagination) also into kindergartens and schools. For this I have initiated the childrens' books' series *I Am So Fantastic*. They are read-together books, and they also address the inner child in the adult. The first volumes are *You are Extraordinary* and *You are Heartful*. Volume 3 will be *You are Natural*. The books have all been tested with children in schools and families.

Unleash your potential and be exceptional!

"You are Extraordinary" is a book for young readers, families, kindergartens and schools. The book tells the great transformation of the butterfly queen Sophia Monarch. Sophia helps to inspire, to discover and to unfold your own powers and possibilities.

"You are Extraordinary" is a read-together-book, a coloring book and an exercise book to strengthen your imagination and self-esteem. Even adults can do the exercises, discovering and letting free their own inner child.

So. we become profoundly ourselves and extraordinary.

About the author

Dr. Alexandra Kleeberg is a psychoanalyst, psychodrama therapist and behavioral therapist. She works in groups to revitalize the self-healing powers and the creative possibilities through embodi-mental imagination. Her great vision is that exercises for self-healing and potential development will be taught in kindergartens and schools. In this way, children can easily and playfully learn to trust their own powers and to unfold them creatively into the world.

www.dralexandrakleeberg.com

ALEXANDRA KLEEBERG

YOU ARE EXTRAORDINARY
POWER TIPS FOR HAPPY KIDS
A READ TOGETHER BOOK FOR SMALL AND TALL

Teach Your Heart to Guide You to Health and Happiness

"You Are Heartful" is a read-together book for families, kindergartens and schools. In this second book of the series, You Are Fantastic, the butterfly queen, Sophia Monarch, explains the sympathetic and the parasympathetic nervous systems symbolized by the lion Simpa and the lioness Pasy. Adventures with Simpa and Pasy show you how to release and transform fear and anger and find balance again. The magic formulas are exercises to energize your life, to calm down, to heal and to play in flow.

Abracadabra!

"You Are Heartful" is also a play book and a colouring book that teaches young readers ways to develop good relationships with their bodies and using the power of imagination to always bounce back into balance.

About the author:

Dr. Alexandra Kleeberg is a psychoanalyst, psychodrama therapist and behavioral therapist. She works in groups to revitalize the self-healing powers and the creative possibilities through embodi-mental imagination. Her great vision is that exercises for self-healing and potential development will be taught in kindergartens and schools.

In this way, children can easily and playfully learn to trust their own powers and to unfold them creatively into the world.

www.evisionpublishing.com

ISBN 978-0-9468-66-99-4

9 780946 586799

ALEXANDRA KLEEBERG

YOU ARE HEARTFUL
ADVENTURES WITH SIMPA AND PASY
A READ TOGETHER BOOK FOR HAPPY KIDS

Printed in the United States
By Bookmasters